Hazel Vaughn Leigh
and the

FORT WORTH BOYS' CLUB

Hazel Vaughn Leigh
and the

❋❋❋❋❋❋❋❋❋❋❋❋❋❋❋❋❋❋❋❋❋❋

FORT WORTH
BOYS' CLUB

❋❋❋❋❋❋❋❋❋❋❋❋❋❋❋❋❋❋❋❋❋❋

by

J'Nell L. Pate

J'nell L. Pate

2000

———— Published for ————

THE FORT WORTH PUBLIC LIBRARY

by

Texas Christian University Press

Copyright © 2000, Fort Worth Public Library

Library of Congress Cataloging-in-Publication Data

Pate, J'Nell L.
  Hazel Vaughn Leigh and the Fort Worth Boys' Club / by J'Nell L. Pate.
    p. cm.
  Includes bibliography references and index.
  ISBN 0-87565-206-9 (alk. paper)
    1. Fort Worth Boys' Club. 2. Leigh, Hazel Vaughn, 1897- I. Title.

HS3321.F67 P37 2000
369.42'092—dc21
[B]

99-047283

Cover and text design by Bill Maize; Duo Design Group

Hazel,

this one's for you.
I would like to think that
you would have liked it.
As always, for Kenneth too!

Dear Reader,

Since it first opened in 1901, the Fort Worth Public Library has made many valuable friends, Hazel Vaughn Leigh among them. Mrs. Leigh was a magnanimous supporter of the library and donated her personal papers to our archival collection in Genealogy and Local History. The gift of her papers made this book possible.

In 1935, the City of Fort Worth's Juvenile Department issued a report documenting the rise in "boy-perpetrated delinquency." The report made headlines. Mrs. Leigh was the leader of a handful of concerned and dedicated citizens who founded the Fort Worth Boys' Club in response to the report. The club's building on Northwest 20th Street and Ellis Avenue opened in 1937. The creation of the club was credited with greatly reducing juvenile delinquency.

Mrs. Leigh's efforts were later recognized in 1993 by the North Fort Worth Historical Society with their prestigious Life Achievement Award. She was also the recipient of an award from the Fort Worth Commission on the Status of Women.

It is our deepest desire and hope that the publication of this book will also aptly reward her efforts as a friend of the library and the city but, more importantly, a friend to young people. We applaud her efforts.

Sincerely,
Gleniece A. Robinson
Library Director

CONTENTS

✼✼✼✼✼✼✼✼✼✼ PREFACE ✼✼✼✼✼✼✼✼✼✼

*I*n telling Hazel Vaughn Leigh's story, I was aware that she was gone and would not know what was said about her. Conversely, some of the folks with whom she clashed at the end were still around to read the book and see themselves portrayed. I did not know Mrs. Leigh, but I know some of the people she worked with and confronted; I've become acquainted with many more during the course of this research. As a historian, I have tried to be fair to all sides and present the truth as I see it.

Many people knew Mrs. Leigh personally for a number of years, but perhaps they did not know the complete story of her life. From her own records, including the minutes of the Fort Worth Boys' Club, Inc., the Fort Worth Boys' Club Endowment Fund, Inc., and the Fort Worth Boys' Club Council, Inc., an accurate account can be pieced together.

This is her story as she intended to write it but waited until she was too old to do it. Her records were kept in good order, with handwritten annotations. Obviously, she could have added personal anecdotes and reminiscences. She would know the very day and situation when she met her husband, which I have been unable to find, and she would remember many words that were said between them through the years, words that I could not know.

However, the story of the Panther Boys' Club, the Fort Worth Boys' Club, the national boys' club movement—and the local and national boys' and girls' clubs merger that she opposed—was documented. Hazel Vaughn Leigh's involvement in these organizations for more than half a century may surprise many.

As I researched, I became concerned that too much attention may focus on Hazel Vaughn Leigh for the work at the Fort Worth Boys' Club and not enough credit be given to the selfless and dedicated service performed by all the other ladies, their husbands, and the men of the Kiwanis Club of North Fort Worth. We must not forget that Dr. Abe Greines served as president of the Fort Worth Boys' Club, Inc., Board for thirty-six years. If Hazel was the "mother" of all those boys through the years, Dr. Greines certainly was the "father," even if (and probably because) neither of them had any children of their own!

Mrs. Bert (Minnie) Weekley gave many hours of service for nearly forty years as an officer on the board of both the Boys' Club and the ladies' Fort Worth Boys' Club Council. Many more men and women gave numerous hours of service. This may be Hazel's story, but the establishment and operation of the Fort Worth Boys' Club was a group effort. By her energy, personality, and organizational skills, Hazel tended to stand out. Add to that her longevity and the interest she maintained, and history cannot help but forever associate the name of Hazel Vaughn Leigh with the establishment of the Fort Worth Boys' Club on the North Side of Fort Worth.

Numerous people helped me tremendously as I worked on this project. Ken Hopkins, manager of the genealogy and local history section of the Fort Worth Public Library, accepted the records from Mrs. Leigh and assisted me in research. Also helpful to me were Max Hill, assistant manager and senior librarian, and Shirley Apley, senior librarian, both of the genealogy and local history section. At the University of Texas at Arlington's Special Collections, Katherine "Kit" Goodwin cheerfully brought out the *Fort Worth Star-Telegram* Collection. Billy Sills, who is retired from the Fort Worth Public Schools, maintains the archives for the schools and checked on some things for me there.

Mrs. Wanda Gibson let me borrow some Panther Boys' Club letters and other records belonging to her aunt, Mrs. Martha Justice Ball, and then donated them to the Fort Worth Public Library. Preston Geren, Jr., and his secretary, Judy Wilson, answered numerous questions and let me have the nurses' log of Mrs. Leigh's last few months. I appreciate Eileen Snyder, Paul Koeppe, Preston Geren, Jr., and Joe Cordova, the executive director of the Boys' and Girls' Clubs of Greater Fort Worth, for reading the book in manuscript form.

Of course, the interpretation of the records detailing the life of Hazel Vaughn Leigh is my own.

CHAPTER 1

❦❦❦❦❦❦❦❦❦❦❦❦❦❦❦❦❦❦❦❦❦❦❦❦❦❦❦❦❦❦

Growing Up in Fort Worth

When the night nurse arrived with a rose and a birthday card, Hazel knew that the people who cared for her had not forgotten her special day on the morrow. She would be ninety-seven years old July 27, 1994. Sure enough, the following morning flower arrangements and telephone calls began coming from several friends. Judy Wilson, Preston Geren, Jr.'s secretary, arrived at 1:00 p.m. with a cake and balloons.

The day's activities tired Hazel, so she was dozing at 5:10 p.m. when Bill Burklow called from Houston to wish her a happy birthday. When she took the telephone, Hazel at first seemed disoriented, but then she was happy to hear from Billy. Little Billy Burklow, one of her boys, epitomized the reason she and the ladies and the men of the Kiwanis Club had started the Boys' Club back in 1935 on the North Side. During those Depression years, little boys like Billy needed clothing and a place to go after school while their parents worked. Even though Burklow became a prominent businessman in Houston, Hazel always thought of him as seven-year-old "little Billy Burklow." Through the nearly sixty years since those early days Bill always kept in touch. A woman with no children of her own and no nieces or nephews, Hazel considered the youngsters of the Fort Worth Boys' Club "her" boys.

When the nurse checked the mail box of Hazel's Trinity Terrace retirement apartment, it contained many birthday cards. Bill and Evelyn Burklow's card was there too.

Preston Geren, Jr., called in the evening. His mother-in-law, Mrs. Charles Lupton, had been one of the ladies who helped Mrs. Leigh in the early years with the Fort Worth Boys' Club. Consequently, with really no one else left to do it, he was overseeing Hazel's care.[1]

Mrs. Leigh had often told her nurses that she was "writing a book soon" and that she needed "all of her papers together."

"I don't think my health is going to hold out until I get this finished," Mrs. Leigh told her nurse.

"Get what finished?"

"A history book."[2]

Indeed, Hazel intended to write her life story and that of the Fort Worth Boys' Club. For years she saved clippings, minutes of meetings, documents from the court cases, letters, often writing in the margins in a shaky hand such notes as "That is untrue!"

She wanted to tell her story but, finally realizing that she probably would not be able to do it, she called the genealogy and local history section of the Fort Worth Public Library. After several meetings with manager Ken Hopkins, she agreed on November 1, 1991, to donate all of her papers to the library, releasing them over the next four years. Her will requested that the records be used to write the book that she had become too feeble to write.

Notice should be taken that Hazel was over ninety-four years old before she realized she really could not do it and that getting the book done remained on her mind near her birthday nearly three years later. As those who knew her could testify, Hazel Vaughn Leigh did not give up on things easily.

Hazel's roots in Tarrant County stretched even farther back than her ninety-seven-plus years. Her maternal great-grandfather, John Wiley Chapman, at age thirty-two came to Hunt County, Texas, with his wife, the former Martha Ann Davis, and their children in 1845. Although he moved around a bit, he eventually settled in the 1850s in southern Tarrant County on what later became Oak Grove Road, a place Hazel herself would later own and call home.

Chapman owned several families of slaves whom he had purchased from a Mr. Handley. One of the slaves was named Lewis, to whom Chapman later deeded thirty acres for diligent service. After Mr. and Mrs. Chapman were gone, Lewis Chapman and his wife invited their former owner's granddaughter Bess and her husband Sam Vaughn (Hazel's parents) every summer to their farm near Kennedale and cooked dinner for them. Hazel remembered that the former slaves stood at the end of the table and watched the family eat the meal, which was served on a white tablecloth that Mrs. Chapman had given them.[3]

Lewis's own daughter named Bess took care of Hazel when she was young. She never had to pick up her own clothes, which may explain why she was a bit messy as an adult.[4]

Hazel's great-grandfather Chapman, although overage, served in the Confederacy and became a colonel. His main task was delivering cattle to soldiers. Two sons also served, but one died of measles. After the Civil War, Chapman bought and sold a lot of real estate in the county, and in 1865 deeded fifteen acres to the Presbyterian Church for Forest Hill Cemetery. Chapman also served as a county commissioner for several terms.

Chapman's daughter Mattie married a wealthy rancher from Clay County, Texas, a Frenchman originally from Montreal, named Seraphine DeCory. They had three children. Elizabeth, or Bessie, born September 15, 1876, would later be the mother of Hazel. When Martha J. "Mattie" DeCory died in 1884 in Henrietta, Mr. and Mrs. Chapman moved there to help raise their grandchildren. Chapman died in 1885, but his wife brought his body back to be buried at Forest Hill. She then returned to Tarrant County with her grandchildren and built a new two-story home on their land in Tarrant County. Mrs. Martha Chapman's other daughter Nannie helped raise the young children until her own marriage to Jack Martin, a school teacher at Mansfield. Unfortunately, Nannie died in 1893 and left a two-year-old daughter named Vera. Great-grandmother Chapman thus accepted another child to raise.[5]

Elizabeth "Bessie" DeCory Vaughn and Samuel Vaughn, Jr., Hazel's parents. Courtesy Fort Worth Public Library.

Martha Chapman's granddaughter, Bessie DeCory (daughter of Mattie), attended Polytechnic College (later Texas Wesleyan) in 1892. She married Sam Vaughn in 1893, and they lived with Mrs. Chapman. Martha Chapman died September 3, 1894, and was buried beside her husband in Forest Hill. This left the young couple Sam and Bessie Vaughn living in the big Chapman place, raising Bessie's two younger DeCory brothers, their own young son Howard—born September 6, 1894—and three-year-old Vera Martin, whose father Jack continued to live there too. Sam and Bessie's second child, Hazel Elizabeth, was born July 27, 1897.

Her father's family, the Vaughns, were early Texas pioneers as well. Her grandfather, Samuel Vaughn, and his wife, the former Mary Elizabeth Adams, came to Tarrant County in 1871 from Georgia and bought land where Everman is now located. His namesake, Hazel's father, Samuel Harrison Vaughn, Jr., was born June 18, 1873.[6]

Hazel is three and one-half and brother Howard six-years-old in this photo. Courtesy Fort Worth Public Library.

Hazel's Grandfather Vaughn had been born in Franklin County, Georgia, on January 9, 1836. During the Civil War he served three years in the Fifteenth Georgia Regiment, surviving at Bull Run, Gettysburg, and Sharpsburg. He farmed in Georgia before deciding to come to Texas, arriving in a covered wagon with two other families, the Youngs and Davises.[7]

Hazel's parents listed their occupations as "farmer" and "housewife" on her birth certificate. Sam was one of nine children, so when all of them married and had families, the Vaughn clan would gather at the senior Sam Vaughn's for Sunday dinner or Christmas. Hazel enjoyed playing with all her Chambers, Sewell, Powell, and Vaughn cousins. Sometimes on holidays like July 4 the Vaughn clan would drive into Fort Worth from the country to Hermann Park on the North Side. Hazel also remembered touring one of the new Armour or Swift meat-packing plants as a child.[8]

When Theodore (Teddy) Roosevelt came to Fort Worth on April 8, 1905, Sam Vaughn was determined that his children would see the president. He loaded the family into a two-horse surrey, and they drove into town from the farm.

"Daddy passed everybody on the way. He was quite a cutup and would holler to everybody. 'We're going to see the flea on Teddy's back,' he would say."[9]

Twenty thousand people greeted the president as he arrived at the Texas & Pacific terminal early in the morning. Crowds lined the streets as he rode in a carriage to Ninth and Throckmorton, where he planted a tree on the grounds of the Carnegie Library. He then left for Vernon, Texas, and later Indian Territory, where he engaged in a famous wolf hunt with Tom Waggoner, Burk Burnett, and Quanah Parker.[10]

Decades later, Hazel remembered standing in the rain to see President Theodore Roosevelt visit Fort Worth a second time on Tuesday, March 14, 1911, when he came to speak in the North Side Coliseum.[11]

Hazel would grow up not seeing as much of her Vaughn cousins as she had as a youngster, for in 1905, her parents moved into Fort Worth to a rented house at 1100 Lipscomb, on the corner of Rosedale. Sam and Bessie wanted their children, eleven-year-old Howard and eight-year-old Hazel, to attend city schools. The children were enrolled at DeZavala School on Alston Avenue. In a school picture made that year, the dark-haired, prim and proper Hazel wore glasses.[12]

Hazel in her Sunday best, about eight or nine years old. Courtesy Fort Worth Public Library.

Miss Lula Underwood's second-grade classroom had a high ceiling and traditional connected desks in a row with holes for inkwells in each desk. The twenty-three girls sat on one side of the classroom, and the eighteen boys sat on the other. Howard's fifth grade class had forty-six students.[13]

When Sam and Bessie Vaughn had moved into Fort Worth, Jack Martin and his daughter Vera moved to El Paso. (Vera's mother Nannie and Bessie's mother Mattie were sisters.) Although Vera was really a first cousin to Hazel's mother, she and Hazel had been raised together in their early years and felt like sisters, for Vera was only six years older than Hazel.[14]

Sam Vaughn worked for Axtell Company, a windmill supply business. He would be employed there for thirty-five years before starting his own windmill supply at 715 West Belknap in 1939.[15]

No doubt the Vaughns also wanted to be in the city so they could take Hazel to eye doctors more easily. She suffered what was then called a "dead eye"—a condition that caused the lid of her right eye to droop. It had been injured at birth. Her parents sent her to numerous doctors to get it corrected, but they were told that nothing could be done.

"Now, if she were cross-eyed, we could have corrected that," they were told frequently.

"So I just lived with it," Hazel explained.[16] As a child she was very self-conscious, however.

Sam and Bessie became charter members of the College Avenue Baptist Church when it withdrew from Broadway Baptist, and Sam became an early day choir leader. People met in their home for singing, and Bessie taught Sunday School.[17] "We had to be there when the doors opened," Hazel remembered. She was in Miss Minton's Sunday School class about 1910.[18]

Their grandfather, Sam Vaughn, Sr., died in 1908. To indicate the influence of these early families, Vaughn Boulevard in the Polytechnic area of Fort Worth was named after one of their grandfather's brothers, Freeman Vaughn. Sam inherited some land in Everman from his father, as did his siblings.[19]

The Vaughns later moved to a big two-story house at 2700 Travis Avenue. There Hazel had a friend named Ruby with whom she had tea parties and played other girlhood games, although Hazel was a bit older than Ruby. No doubt Ruby listened to Hazel practicing on the piano, for she had begun taking lessons at "Fort Worth University" located at the corner of Wheeler Street and Cannon Avenue. She finished eighth grade at Eleventh Ward, Alexander Hogg School, and went directly to Central High School, located on Jennings Avenue.[20]

Hazel spent the summer of 1911 in Ysleta, an old Spanish settlement dating from 1681—the oldest town in Texas—located near El Paso. She visited Vera Martin and her father Jack who had homesteaded a ranch at Hueco Tanks. They also owned a small house in town next to the Ysleta Mission church. Only a half dozen or so Anglo families lived in Ysleta, which was predominantly Mexican. Vera would have been nineteen or twenty and Hazel about fourteen, but the young women had much in common. That year Vera met a young man named Tom Duncan whom she married on January 29, 1912. A picture that Hazel probably acquired that summer showed a radiant Vera Martin, wearing a white dress with ruffled bodice and a large white bow in her hair.[21]

CHAPTER 2

✦✦✦✦✦✦✦✦✦✦✦✦✦✦✦✦✦✦✦✦✦✦✦✦✦✦✦✦✦✦✦

Unflappable Flapper

Sixteen-year-old Hazel could hardly contain her excitement as she dressed for the football banquet in the fall of 1913. Her parents were only letting her go because her older brother Howard was on the Central High School team. Also, her parents knew Mr. and Mrs. B. W. Couch, who had agreed to sponsor the event at the Westbrook Hotel. A young men's club called the Isch Ka Bibble Club was holding the event.

Hazel feared that no one would ask her to dance but she need not have worried. As the pretty younger sister of Howard "Shorty" Vaughn, speedy right end on the 1913 Central High School team, she could count on plenty of attention. On the twenty-place dance card that she saved, a young man named Merwyn Barnum signed up for four dances. Scott Townsend signed for two.[1]

Hazel was proud of her brother. Shorty had been captain of the team the previous year but modestly declined the honor again.[2] He was so popular and good looking that girls came over to their house and courted Hazel's friendship just to see Howard. Although three years older, Howard was only a year ahead of Hazel at Central. After graduating from Central in 1914, in the fall he entered Texas Christian University, where he played football for three years and basketball for four. In the *Horned Frog* annual he was called "Shorty the Great."[3]

Howard's years at TCU made Hazel very proud. In the 1915 football season "Shorty" was still playing end. He had a great deal of speed and the ability to receive forward passes. By the 1916 basketball season he was captain of the team and played center. Howard, a Beta Phi in 1917–18, was assistant business manager of the *Horned Frog* in 1918, and graduated that year.[4]

As a teenager in high school, the big attraction for Hazel and her friends was the Majestic Theatre on Saturday afternoons. "For fifty cents you could have a grand time," Hazel said. "You could go to the Majestic or you could go to the picture show, or you could have a sundae." The Majestic in downtown was vaudeville in those days.[5]

Hazel and her friends could ride the streetcar down Hemphill Street to downtown. On a date, if the boy did not have a car, they rode the streetcar. Some of the boys Hazel knew were allowed to have the family car, however. Hazel remembered that Scott Townsend would use his mother's chauffeur and come and pick up Hazel and her friends in the large car. Hazel was dating one of the boys in the group, and the chauffeur would take them to River Crest Country Club.   Hazel remembered wearing floor-length taffeta dresses to the dances at the country club and the Metropolitan Hotel. She was slender, about five feet two, and weighed less than a hundred pounds. "My mother would put tulle all around to cover me up," she recalled.[6] The boys often sent flowers in those days, she added.

Hazel did not have to work while she was in high school. "Girls just didn't work" in those days, she said. Her family hired African American housekeepers—colored help, as they were called then—so Hazel never learned to clean or to cook for herself, the assumption being that she would never need to.

During dates and excursions with her friends, she rode the Ferris wheel at White City, the amusement park on the North Side constructed by Sam Rosen to encourage people from all over the city to use his streetcar line. She and her friends also visited an amusement park in Handley and rode the merry-go-round at Lake Como, another amusement area west of the city.[7]

One of Hazel's classmates at Central High School was Olive Burton. The Burtons lived near Broadway and St. Louis streets, directly south of the Texas & Pacific Railroad terminal downtown. W. G. Burton owned the Burton-Peels Dry Goods Company at Seventh and Main downtown. Later the Burton family moved to a house on Pruitt Street between Eighth Avenue and Fifth. Hazel was invited there after Mrs. Burton helped the girls organize a music and social club. The girls called it the Falcolm Hegbeth Club, which incorporated the first initial of most of the founding members of the club. Hazel was not a founding member, but she was invited to join. She and the girls spent many weekends at slumber parties at the Burton home.

The young ladies' club of eighteen to twenty members always sponsored a dance at River Crest Country Club in May. The broad porch around the ballroom was a "marvelous place" to promenade with one's date between dances.

Social life for the young people generally centered around parties and dances given in each other's homes. Through the club and the young ladies Hazel met, she became a part of Fort Worth's elite social circle. Olive Burton had two older sisters, Nenetta (Netta) and Naomi. Netta was one of six assembly debutantes presented at River Crest Country Club in 1914, and she would later be the second wife of Amon G. Carter. Presented the year before was another of their friends, Pauline Stripling, daughter of W. C. Stripling, who owned a department store in downtown Fort Worth.[8]

When Hazel and her friends in the class of 1915 graduated from Central High School on Jennings Avenue, Hazel, who was still seventeen, graduated cum laude. At the graduation ceremony the girls carried bouquets of red roses. During that season Mrs. Guy Waggoner gave a graduation luncheon for the girls in the Waggoner home on Summit. Another classmate was David Googins, whose father, Joe B. Googins, was president of the Swift and Company meat-packing plant in North Fort Worth. Hazel also attended a party at the Googins home.[9] "I was amazed going from the top floor ballroom to the basement to see an indoor swimming pool," Hazel said. David had a younger sister named Ruth who would later marry Elliot Roosevelt, the son of Franklin D. Roosevelt.[10]

An organization called The Kirmiss, added in 1913 to the stock show, attracted the wealthier families because their daughters were invited to be queens. A separate theme would be selected for each year, and the coliseum would be transformed to comply even though, surprisingly, the themes were not western. Sometimes 7,000 people would crowd into the coliseum on the North Side for the event. Pauline Stripling was queen of the stock show in 1914, and Hazel and others were invited to be in her court. The evening before the grand opening of the stock show, promoters presented an elaborate pageant, during which the queen and her court were named.[11] "We were dressed as sunflowers and followed behind the queen." Later they attended Queen Pauline's reception and dance at the Westbrook Hotel.[12]

About this same time a grand opera came to town, *Carmen*. "I had never seen an opera, so my boyfriend paid $10 apiece and we went, but I couldn't understand it and went to sleep!" Hazel wrote later.[13]

Hazel enjoyed the Falcolm Hegbeth Social Club from 1915 to 1918. The club ended when someone spiked the punch at a dance at River Crest Country Club. Several couples, riding in one car, had a wreck that killed one of the girls.

Another thing that broke up the club was a sermon on "the evils of youth," delivered by the Reverend J. Frank Norris of the First Baptist Church. Hazel said that this same group of young ladies later originated the Junior League.[14]

Hazel and her family did not attend the First Baptist Church and did not really know J. Frank Norris except by reputation. The Vaughns apparently were not the Norris type of strict Baptists. They certainly did not disapprove of dancing, as many Baptists in that era did. Hazel later reminisced that after first moving to Fort Worth "everything circled around the church."

"Later . . . after I got in high school, things changed, you know."[15]

Girls did not graduate from high school and go immediately to college in those days, so even though Howard had done so, Hazel did not. At one point, most likely after her high school graduation, Hazel began dating a young Catholic accountant. She was impressed because "we didn't have many accountants in Fort Worth in those days." He worked for the only accounting firm.

Apparently her Protestant parents were not too happy about her dating a Catholic, even if their own church attendance had slipped somewhat and they were allowing Howard and Hazel to attend dances. She discontinued dating the accountant. There were "such tremendous feelings . . . about Catholics then," she remembered years later.[16]

World War I, or the Great War as people would call it, erupted in Europe in August 1914. Many years later Hazel remembered the day in April 1917 that the United States entered the war and, of course, the day Howard volunteered. Having graduated from TCU in the spring of 1918, he joined and was assigned to the quartermaster department, stationed in San Antonio at Camp Travis. By September 1918 he was a sergeant. The war ended before he saw duty overseas.[17]

As soon as the United States became involved in the war, a military camp named for Jim Bowie of Texas Revolution–Alamo fame was established in Fort Worth. City fathers offered a site for the camp west of town in the addition called Arlington Heights. In fact, Hazel frequently traveled out Arlington Heights Boulevard to the dances at River Crest Country Club. Headquarters for the camp were only a half mile south of the country club, and later the city changed the name of the wide, brick-paved thoroughfare to Camp Bowie Boulevard. Construction of the camp was completed by the fall of 1917.

By 1918 when the Spanish influenza spread havoc across the country, officials curtailed visits of Camp Bowie soldiers to downtown. Servicemen could

Howard Vaughn's Army photo, 1918. He was in the Quartermaster Department in San Antonio during World War I. Courtesy Fort Worth Public Library.

visit downtown but could not take part in any large gathering. To the chagrin of Hazel and her friends, most of the social and entertainment programs planned for the soldiers had to be canceled.[18] Later, Hazel remembered the day the armistice was signed, November 11, 1918. "Everybody went downtown, and the streets were full of people parading up and down."[19]

Sam and Bess Vaughn apparently let Hazel freely enjoy her parties and social activities in the two or three years after graduation from high school. Perhaps they believed that she would marry soon, as many young ladies did. Bess herself had married Sam when she was only seventeen. But in Hazel's day the Great War had carried many young men off to the service, disrupting everyone's lives.

Hazel persuaded her parents to let her get a job at Camp Bowie as the war was ending and the camp was closing. For several months she worked in Captain Hulsey's department filing personnel records. When Hazel picked up the telephone at the camp, an operator would ask, "Number please." There were only three exchanges in the city: Lamar, Rosedale, and Prospect.[20]

In January 1920, she began a job at E. M. Daggett Elementary School. One of her duties was to handle the truancy cases with the city juvenile officer. "I discovered then that there were just about as many problems as there were boys."[21]

Whether or not Hazel realized it at the time, she had grown to adulthood during the Progressive Era, which stretched from the 1890s to the end of World War I. She was a product of the period of social change and political ferment influenced by Theodore Roosevelt and Woodrow Wilson in which reform, trust busting, and the social gospel were the order of the day. Individual salvation—stressed by J. Frank Norris and the Baptists—was not enough, said the social gospel advocates, who called for major social reforms to achieve a more "equitable, a more Christian society." Hazel would be influenced by the reform movement.[22]

In 1923 Hazel was promoted to secretary to the principal of E. M. Daggett. While she was really too young to take part in some of the society events of young matrons, Hazel may have taken note that the Fort Worth Woman's Club was founded in 1923 with headquarters in a former residence in the 1300 block of Pennsylvania Avenue. She would be a part of it later.[23]

Hazel bobbed her hair, shortened her skirts, and began wearing silk stockings like the other enlightened young women of the 1920s. After all, the Eighteenth Amendment outlawing alcohol was quickly followed by the Nineteenth, giving women the right to vote. In 1920, Hazel was twenty-three and old enough to vote. Because the South was solidly Democratic and her mother Bess later active in Democratic politics, her first vote for president most likely was for the Democratic candidate James M. Cox and his vice-presidential running mate Franklin D. Roosevelt. Of course, the winners were Republicans Warren G. Harding and Calvin Coolidge.

All that she lacked in her life was a serious romance. Returning prosperity after World War I and the excitement of the Texas oil boom brought Grover Cleveland Leigh into her life.

❦❦❦❦❦❦❦❦❦❦❦❦❦❦❦❦❦❦❦❦❦❦❦❦❦❦❦❦❦❦❦❦❦❦❦

CHAPTER 3

Grover! Grover!

An oil boom in Texas that began during World War I promised increased prosperity even when the military began cutbacks. Several towns about 150 miles west of Fort Worth, in the city's market area, became booming oil towns by 1917 or shortly thereafter—Ranger, Burkburnett, Cisco, Eastland, Breckenridge, and Desdemona. Hazel knew that Burkburnett was named after Anne Burnett's grandfather and located near his 6666 Ranch. (Anne would be Mrs. Guy Waggoner by 1922.) Fort Worth attracted the trade from the oil boom.[1]

By 1918 eighty percent of the oil pipelines in the state connected to Fort Worth, which translated into 3,116 miles of pipe. During the next year, twelve new refineries opened or were under construction. Fort Worth businessmen built new buildings downtown to house the offices of all these new companies. By 1920 the population of the city was growing by 5,000 per month because 500 oil companies and fifty-two oil-field supply businesses called Fort Worth home. Obviously, some of these would be "fly-by-night" and disappear quickly, but the excitement generated by all the activity was contagious. The ten railroads with connections into the city stayed busy hauling pipe and other oil-field equipment, as well as the cattle trade, which had brought them to the city near the turn of the century.[2]

Thus when war veteran and Texas Christian University alumni Howard "Shorty" Vaughn returned home from the service, he had no trouble obtaining his job with National Supply Company, which sold oil-field equipment. Most likely, through his job he encountered employees of Empire Oil and through that connection met Grover Cleveland Leigh.

Grover was the youngest of nine children born to John Reed Leigh and his wife, the former Mary Carolyn Davis, who were married November 30, 1868, in Jerseyville, Illinois.

Grover Cleveland Leigh,
age thirty-four for his
wedding photograph.
Courtesy Fort Worth
Public Library.

Born in Raymond, Illinois, on August 7, 1888, Grover was named after President Grover Cleveland who in 1888 was seeking re-election. [3]

Grover was only eighteen when his father died on February 2, 1907. The record for Grover is blank for the next five years, but on October 12, 1912, he joined the army at Fort Logan, Colorado, for a three-year enlistment. He began learning to use the radio and Morse code as a telegraph operator and was promoted to private first class February 16, 1913. The Army transferred him to Alaska that June where he served until July 4, 1915; he was discharged in Seattle in November, having served in Company C of the Signal Corps. His military record described him as five feet five inches tall, with light blue eyes, dark blond hair, a ruddy complexion, and an "Excellent" character. Returning to civilian life, Grover got a job with Empire Gas and Fuel Company in Oklahoma in 1916. After the United States became involved in World War I, Grover re-enlisted June 14, 1918, and served until December 9 of that year.[4]

After the war, Grover returned to the same oil company for which he had worked prior to his enlistment, Empire. A New York financier named Henry L. Doherty in 1912 had purchased several small Kansas and Oklahoma oil and gas companies and merged them into one with headquarters in Bartlesville. The company's primary interest in its early years was the production and transmission of natural gas. Bartlesville by 1916 had become the center of a field containing more than 21,000 wells. In April 1919, in conjunction with the Masonic Lodge, the Empire Company dedicated a nine-story office building, the largest in Oklahoma at the time. The Empire Gas and Fuel Company rented the basement, ground floor, and six stories of offices for five years at $53,000 per year.[5]

Out of twenty-eight interstate pipeline companies, by net investment in pipelines, Empire ranked ninth in 1920. The expanding company created North Texas and West Texas divisions.[6]

Empire sent Grover C. Leigh to Texas in 1919. Just when he met Howard Vaughn and Hazel Vaughn is not clear. They may have been dating and then decided to marry fairly quickly when he received notice that he was being transferred back to Bartlesville. Hazel, the former socialite, did not plan a big wedding with showers and parties. Of course, by then she was almost a spinster at age twenty-five, with most of her friends already married. Instead, she married at home with only family present, and the Vaughns sent the following announcement to friends:

Mr. & Mrs. Samuel H. Vaughn
announce the marriage of their
daughter Hazel to Mr. Grover C. Leigh
on Monday April the thirtieth 1923
Fort Worth, Texas.

A card inside said, "At home Hotel Maire, Bartlesville, Okla."[7]

Hazel's wedding photo in the *Fort Worth Star-Telegram* shows a slightly smiling, beautiful young lady with short, very dark hair.[8]

Once the newlyweds arrived in Bartlesville, the Empire office staff gave them a present, apparently some sort of cooking implement, with the following verse attached:

To our most beloved Grover:
Since your roving days are over,
and you've copped a loving little wife, at last.
Please accept this useful token
for your bachelor bonds are broken
And your restaurant and luncheon days are past.
Now this gift——'tis quite a dandy,
And your wife will find it handy,
for it cooks the cakes and coffee with a bang.
So as you lick your breakfast platter,
Use your choicest bit of chatter
To convey to her "Best Wishes From the Gang."[9]

Because both their birthdays were in August, Grover was nearly thirty-five and Hazel nearly twenty-six when they married April 30. They moved from their temporary quarters at the Hotel Maire to rooms at 410 Wyandotte Street

Hazels's wedding portrait that appeared in the Fort Worth Star-Telegram *April 30, 1923, when she and Grover married. Hazel was twenty-five-years old and Grover thirty-four. Courtesy Fort Worth Public Library.*

in Bartlesville. Grover worked in the oil production department and saw a great deal of the fancy new offices of the Empire Companies.

For Hazel it was the first time she had lived away from her parents—except for that three-month visit in El Paso—the first home away from Fort Worth, and the first time she did not have a maid to pick up after her. No record has been left of what she did with her days in Bartlesville, or if she was homesick. Many years later, living back in Fort Worth, Hazel visited and kept in touch with friends she had made during this brief sojourn in Bartlesville.[10]

Grover soon was offered a job with Marland Oil Company, which was expanding to California, and he accepted. By early 1925 Grover and Hazel were living in a boarding house in San Francisco at 260 McAllister Street, which was in an area of homes built in the late nineteenth century for middle- and upper-middle-class families. They lived only two blocks off Market Street where Grover could catch a streetcar and go several blocks toward the Bay to the offices of Marland Oil at 200 Bush.[11]

San Francisco in 1925 would have been an exciting place for a young couple to live. Both autos and streetcars traveled on the streets; motion picture theaters nestled among the neighborhood shops and stores of Market and Mission streets near where the Leighs lived. Residents in their neighborhood, the Mission District, were one-fourth foreign-born and three-fourths of foreign parentage, mostly Irish and German. Most, like Grover and Hazel, did not have cars.[12]

She probably read one of the two morning newspapers after Grover left for work. The *San Francisco Chronicle* claimed to be the "Leading Newspaper of the Pacific Coast," and had moved to its new building at Fifth and Mission streets only a year or two before Grover and Hazel arrived in San Francisco. In walking excursions to Market and Mission, they probably passed the building frequently. Perhaps that close proximity gave Hazel the idea to apply for a job. It was only about five blocks from their rooming house, and Hazel grew tired of sitting around in those small rooms.

Hazel knew that Marland Oil Company did not want wives of its employees to work. Consequently, she did not tell Grover that she had applied for a job at the *Chronicle*. She did not even give the newspaper her correct name. She was "Mrs. Brown." Hazel got a job in classified ads. After six months her accuracy, dedication, and organizational skills had moved her to "Classified

Advertising Manager" for the *Chronicle*, with thirty-four employees working under her. Fortunately, she could leave the rooming house each morning after Grover left and arrive home each evening before his own commute by street-car from the downtown offices. If on a few occasions she was not there when he arrived, hopefully, a package or two grabbed on the way home would convince him she had been out shopping. Somehow, after six months of Hazel's "moonlighting," Grover finally caught on. Her blooming career as a newspaperwoman came to an abrupt halt, for the company did not approve.[13]

At one point, Hazel came home to Fort Worth on a visit, and she and her mother drove back to San Francisco in a Model T Ford. At Needles, California, some people refused to let two women strike out alone in a car across the desert; Hazel and her mother left in the middle of the night without telling anyone. They drove on a plank road, crossing the desert in the cool of the night rather than the heat of the day.[14]

Hazel found other things to do in San Francisco. She joined a San Francisco chapter of the Daughters of the Confederacy. On her mother's side with the Chapmans and her father's with the Vaughns, she qualified. Hazel also learned about the Columbia Park Boys' Club in the Mission District. She later told people that her first interest in boys' club work began in San Francisco.[15]

The Columbia Park Boys' Club, founded in 1894 by former military man Major Sidney Peixotto, was first located in a two-story frame building at Seventh and Harrison Streets across from a dilapidated city square called Columbia Park. It was the first boys' club established on the West Coast. Peixotto explained, "I realized that what they needed more than anything else was association and training, and vigorous methods by which they would be dragged from their comatose state and unhealthful and narrow surroundings into an atmosphere of vigor and life and uplifting influences." The Major eliminated money as dues because he wanted to create a "spirit of personal giving and personal work."[16]

When the original club burned in the 1906 earthquake and fire, a new site at 458 Guerrero Street was chosen. The building had a center compound for drills, a large, well-equipped gym and stages, rehearsal rooms, lecture halls, handicraft rooms, and a printing office. Major Peixotto also had arranged summer camps for the boys. Even Jane Addams of Chicago's Hull-House praised Major Peixotto's Columbia Park Boys' Club.[17]

Unfortunately, the Leighs' sojourn in colorful San Francisco came to an end, perhaps because Marland Oil Company was ending as well. J. P. Morgan, who had lent Ernest Marland the money to expand, kept acquiring Marland stock until he had control. Morgan then planned to merge Marland with Continental Oil Company (now Conoco), but Marland fought it. Consequently, in 1928 Marland was ousted from his own company; then in 1929 Marland and Continental merged.[18]

At about the same time that Marland Oil of Ponca City, Oklahoma, was expanding to California, the company organized a Texas branch headquartered first in Houston, then in Fort Worth. W. A. "Monty" Moncrief, who had been in the accounting office in Ponca City, became executive vice president of the Marland Oil Company of Texas, having been with the company ten years. John E. Farrell, who had worked in the lease department in Ponca City, also moved to Fort Worth in 1926, when the company opened its Fort Worth office. After the forced merger of the company with Continental and ouster of their friend and former employer Ernest Marland, both Moncrief and Farrell resigned. Each started his own oil company and began buying leases in East and West Texas.[19]

One of Marland's close friends, William Hartman McFadden, had joined him in business much earlier and had served as vice president of Marland Refining and executive vice president of Marland Oil. In 1928 he too left Marland Oil to combine several employee royalty companies into Southland Royalty Company, based in Fort Worth.[20]

By 1926 Grover and Hazel were back in Fort Worth living at 2700 Travis Avenue with Hazel's parents. Grover obviously knew all the Marland employees who had come to the city and those who would migrate within the next couple of years. Hazel met some of them too because she recruited them later to help with the Fort Worth Boys' Club, especially the Farrells. Even a Continental official, Horace B. Simcox, who became assistant general production manager when Continental took over Marland, later supported the boys' club when his wife became active. Simcox arrived in Fort Worth in 1934 as division general superintendent of Continental Oil.[21]

Back in Fort Worth, Hazel could keep up with local society news without having to get it secondhand from her mother's letters or the newspaper clippings she sometimes had sent. Hazel also entered society with her mother's help. She entertained guests at a bridge luncheon in honor of Miss Elizabeth Evans of Ottumwa, Iowa, who was the guest of her aunt, Mrs. A. L. Shuman. Hazel hosted eleven tables of players on a Monday afternoon in the Sun Parlour of the Women's Club. Mrs. Vaughn helped Hazel entertain.[22]

Hazel also made Genevieve Papineau's "Just Between Us" society column in a local newspaper: "In Tune with Spring is the dashing cape costume in that very new toast shade, worn by Mrs. Grover Leigh, who also sports a flattering face shading chapeau in matching hue."[23]

Grover worked for Royal Manufacturing and Welding Company of Texas on South Main Street in 1926 and 1927. After he left that job Hazel worked as a telephone solicitor for the *Fort Worth Press*, probably citing her experience on the San Francisco *Chronicle* to help her get the job.[24]

Grover worked for a while as an investigator for the Secret Service and then switched to politics and law enforcement. In 1928 when James R. "Red"Wright first ran for sheriff of Tarrant County, Grover served as his campaign manager. After Wright won the election, he appointed Grover deputy sheriff.[25]

As the wife of a deputy sheriff, Hazel got to do some interesting things. The two were invited to a barbecue on Friday May 20, 1932, at Camp Wolters in

Unidentified sheriff's deputies with Grover Leigh, on right, about 1930. Courtesy Fort Worth Public Library.

Mineral Wells. The Mineral Wells Bar Association, the Dallas Bar Association, and the Fort Worth and Tarrant County Bar Associations hosted the event. The invitation said, "Bring your wife along."[26] Grover was invited to a party at the Haltom Farm and to several big parties at Amon Carter's Shady Oaks Farm. Carter was then married to his second wife, Hazel's friend, Nenetta Burton.[27]

"I never saw so much food as he'd have at those parties," Hazel said. "He always gave one at New Years time." In August 1929, Amon Carter even gave a barbecue and watermelon party at Shady Oaks Farm for Grover, possibly making him an honoree with other law enforcement officers.[28]

Prohibition enforcement and the deepening Depression presented problems in law enforcement for the sheriff's department. At 3:00 p.m. on February 18, 1930, there was a run on the First National Bank of Fort Worth. Two weeks earlier the Texas National Bank had collapsed because of bad loans, and many people lost money. Consequently, as a large group of people gathered at First National demanding their money, panicked bank officers called in Sheriff Red Wright and a posse of deputies. Most likely Grover was one of these. Texas Ranger Captain Tom Hickman and city police came as well. Sheriff Wright mingled with the crowd, handing out free hot dogs someone had provided. Amon Carter, who got up from a sickbed to lend his support, paid for cheese sandwiches, and someone ordered donuts and coffee. Carter said, "This is the safest bank in the world and you'll soon find it out." An orchestra played "Home Sweet Home" to help settle the crowd. Carter announced that bank passbooks were good for free admission to the Majestic Theatre, and 200 people left the milling crowd to go see William Boyd in "Officer O'Brien," a talkie.

W. T. Waggoner, Guy Waggoner's father, made a speech to the crowd, holding up his right arm and pledging that the depositors would "not lose a single dollar in this bank. I will sell every cow and every oil well if necessary to pay for any money you lose here." Bank officers and other city officials were relieved when bank officials arrived with a $6,750,000 advance from the Federal Reserve Bank in Dallas. By 8:00 p.m. or so the crisis was over, and the crowd dispersed.[29]

Then at noon on August 9, 1930, a man named Nathan Monroe Martin, age thirty, walked into the Stockyards National Bank and asked for $10,000. He carried a bottle of nitroglycerin in a satchel and dropped it, killing himself and a bank teller.[30] Hazel must have wondered if Grover's salary of $2,400 per year as chief deputy sheriff was worth all the long hours and extra danger.[31]

While Grover worked his long hours, Hazel began to go her own way. In April 1931, she was confirmed as a member of St. Andrews Episcopal Church at Tenth and Lamar in downtown Fort Worth, but Grover was not. That fall she enrolled in a public speaking course at TCU. The registrar's office mailed her report card for the fall semester, 1931–1932, to Mr. Grover Leigh. Hazel made a B.[32]

Grover remained in the sheriff's department until Sheriff Wright decided to seek the federal marshal's job for the Northern District of Texas. Wright was appointed to the position and was sworn in September 1, 1933. The new federal marshal could have twelve deputies who had to be approved in Washington. Grover resigned as deputy sheriff to become a deputy U.S. marshal and took office November 17, 1933.[33]

A couple of events in December 1933 give a possible preview of things to come in Hazel and Grover's relationship. Nationwide prohibition ended on December 5, 1933. Hazel and Grover and three or four other couples "went to town and had the best time because it was just a sightseeing event to us to see what was happening and we went every place that we could, night clubs and so forth, to see what was happening." They "all thought they could drink the town dry that night."[34] Three weeks later, they attended a dance at the Fort Worth Club to signal the end of the Depression. (Or so everyone hoped!) In the program of dances, fourteen dances plus four extras, Grover did not dance a single dance with Hazel. Unless the rule was that no husband could dance with his own wife at this party or he was working, something appeared to be wrong.[35]

Indeed it was. Grover was an alcoholic, but Hazel did not want her friends to know. When the couple came back to Fort Worth from San Francisco, they lived with her parents at 2700 Travis Avenue. On his salary as first a deputy sheriff and then a deputy U.S. marshal, they surely could have afforded their own place. Because of Grover's drinking, Hazel quite possibly came home first from San Francisco to her parents and Grover left his job two years before the Marland Company actually folded and followed his wife. From the time they arrived back in Fort Worth in 1926 until about 1938 they lived with her parents. Some stories surfaced that they sometimes did not speak and only communicated through Hazel's mother, Bess Vaughn.[36]

Things became extremely strained.

CHAPTER 4

❦❦❦❦❦❦❦❦❦❦❦❦❦❦❦❦❦❦❦❦❦❦❦❦❦❦❦❦❦❦

Panther Boys' Club

Despite the Depression, by the mid-1930s Hazel's father Sam Vaughn had worked for the Axtell Windmill Company for about thirty years and was doing well. Consequently, in 1930 the family moved from a leased home on Travis Avenue to their own two-story cream brick home at 1941 Forest Park Boulevard. Hazel and Grover moved too, but their relationship did not improve.

Even if the staunch Baptist beliefs of the Vaughns' early years in Fort Worth had bent a little to let Hazel and Howard attend all those dances, Sam and Bess apparently still did not approve of divorce. Bess tried to maintain the communication channels between Hazel and Grover.

Because Bess was involved in Woman's Club and charity work, Hazel joined too, with all the energies a young matron in her mid-thirties possessed. No children had blessed the marriage, so Hazel felt at loose ends and needed something to do. Several of Bess's high society friends had joined a ladies' auxiliary of the Panther Boys' Club, located in downtown Fort Worth, so Hazel attended with her mother. She remembered the Columbia Park Boys' Club in San Francisco. Hazel did not yet know the history of the boys' club movement, but she was slowly taking the steps with her mother that would later make her an authority.

The nationwide boys' club movement apparently began in 1860 with a club in Hartford, Connecticut. Three young women in that city for several years supervised a self-governing group of boys known as the "Dashaway Club." The club sponsored games, music, dramatics, and dancing. The club disbanded during the Civil War and donated its library fund of $1,000 to the Free Public Library of the city.

The boys' club in Salem, Massachusetts, established in 1869 as the "Salem Fraternity," maintained uninterrupted service into the twentieth century.

New Bedford, Connecticut, in 1870 organized a "Union for Good Works" and maintained a games room and reading room for boys. In New Haven, Connecticut, a group of women—Mrs. Leigh underlined "women" in pencil in her copy of the national boys' club history—known as the "willing workers" opened club rooms for boys in 1872.[1]

The Boys' Club of New York apparently first used the name "boys' club" in 1876. Then in 1906 some fifty boys' clubs banded together to establish a national organization called the Federated Boys' Clubs. Jacob Riis, one of New York's great social workers, was elected president and served until 1909. In 1915 the name changed to Boys' Clubs Federation. In 1931 the word "Federation" was dropped, and the name became the Boys' Clubs of America, Inc.[2]

For nearly six decades this name described the organization that loosely united the boys' club movement, with each club being an autonomous, private, non-profit group. Individual clubs formed associations with groups in their own communities such as the Elks, Lions, Moose, Veterans of Foreign Wars, Jaycees, American Legion, Kiwanis, and even the CIO.[3]

The first boys' club in Dallas apparently was the Red Shield Boys' Club maintained in the 1940s by the Salvation Army at 2102 Browder Street. By 1965 there was a West Dallas Boys' Club. In quick order, a Turnkey Boys Club, an Oak Cliff Boys Club, and East Dallas Club followed. Later a Mesquite Club and a Grand Prairie Club began operations, and even more were added later.[4]

The Panther Boys' Club was organized in Fort Worth about the time that Hazel and Grover returned from San Francisco. L. B. Price, a multi-millionaire merchant from Greenwich, Connecticut, was the guest speaker at the annual banquet of the Rotarians at the Union Gospel Mission in Fort Worth in early February 1926. He told the two hundred Fort Worth businessmen attending that he "would be afraid to meet his maker without sharing his riches with the 'underdogs' of life." D. Van Gieson of Fort Worth had invited Price to speak to the group; Van Gieson was regional manager of Price's dozens of L. B. Price Mercantile Company stores in Texas, Arizona, and Colorado, and had been working for Price for thirty-three years.[5]

Price brought with him to Fort Worth C. J. Atkinson, director of the National Boys' Clubs Federation who urged citizens to start such a club local-ly. Price spoke up and volunteered to donate the first $1,000 to get the project started. Price concluded his remarks and his appeal to the men and then sat down. His face turned ashen; he crumpled in his chair, and died without saying another word.[6]

With so dramatic an event spurring the men on, they felt compelled to carry through. Throughout the coming months Rotary Club members and others worked to organize the club. They sold bonds at $10 each to raise $10,000 to start. At a luncheon on September 20, 1926, the men declared the club organized, elected an attorney, W. H. Slay, president of the board, and named K. S. Ickes the club's executive director. Dr. Wilmer Allison was president of the Rotary Club at that time.[7]

The first clubhouse opened on November 17, 1926, at 111 1/2 East Third Street, downtown, on the second floor of the building. The men first named their club the L. B. Price Memorial Boys' Club. They called it Price Boys' Club, then News Boys' Club, and then settled on Panther Boys' Club as its permanent name. It apparently became the second oldest boys' club in Texas.[8]

Membership at first consisted of newsboys and others in the immediate downtown neighborhood of the club. For the first big party for the boys, a Christmas party, Northern Texas Traction Company, the streetcar company, donated a tree, lights, and decorations. Ladies involved were Mrs. Henry B. Trigg and Mrs. W. H. Slay, wife of the PBC board president. The women solicited donations so that each boy received a half-pound of Pangburns' chocolate candy, a striped candy cane, an apple, and an orange. At the party Myrtle Dockery School of Expression entertained the boys. The club moved to better quarters in 1928 in the Weatherford Street Methodist Church building.[9]

One of the first employees hired to work at the club was a young lady of eighteen. Martha Justice, who had graduated from Central High School the previous spring, became the secretary who did whatever needed to be done. Martha was five foot two, vivacious, outgoing and pretty. Her family had moved from Illinois to Fort Worth when Martha was only one year old because her father was a railroad engineer. She had a sister named Margaret three years older than she.[10]

By January 1, 1927, Fort Worth society matrons formed a ladies' auxiliary for the Panther Boys' Club. They selected Mrs. Henry B. Trigg as acting chairman; she appointed a nominating committee to suggest a slate of officers and a board. The ladies organized quickly with Mrs. Slay as president of the PBC

Women's Council. On April 27, 1927, they gave their first banquet to raise money; with the food they prepared they served 100 men to whom they had sold tickets.

Mrs. Slay soon resigned to become state president of the Womens' Auxiliary of her husband's medical association. In May the ladies elected Mrs. Guy Waggoner as president of the Women's Council. This was not the same Mrs. Guy Waggoner who had given the high school graduation party for Hazel and her friends over a decade before. Guy Waggoner was married to the grand-daughter of Samuel Burk Burnett, Anne. That June, Mrs. Waggoner entertained the boys from the club with a picnic and swim at her home on Crestline Road. Neither Hazel nor her mother were on the board.[11]

Community-minded Fort Worth citizens quickly assisted the new Panther Boys' Club. Land on Meandering Road, furnished by the Fort Worth parks department, became a 100–acre camp for the boys that first summer of 1927. Boys could stay two weeks, learn to swim, and enjoy fishing and boating. The cost per child of $8 per day was raised by donations. By the second summer of the camp the boys also raised fruits and vegetables under the direction of a Tarrant County agriculture agent. They hoped to make money by selling the vegetables. A boy could become a stockholder in the venture called "Boyville Gardens" by subscribing $1 stock.[12]

By June 1, 1928, Miss Anne Burnett (who had divorced Guy) became pres-ident of the Women's Council again and led two hundred ladies to sponsor a "Panther Review" at the Pantages Theater in Fort Worth. A matinee Thursday, June 21, two night performances and another matinee Saturday, June 23, filled out the review. Beautiful costumes, dancing, music, a style show, comedy skits all were planned to raise money for the Panther Boys' Club.[13]

Men who were the elite of Fort Worth business and society served as direc-tors of the PBC. The list of directors in 1929 included Amon G. Carter, M. H. Moore, W. C. Stripling, L. A. Boswell, G. W. Haltom, Fritz Lanham, and Mrs. Winfield Scott.[14] Apparently in the next couple of years the PBC ladies' group was not as active as it had been in the beginning. During the year that Mr. J. C. Maxwell was elected president of the PBC board, he asked Mrs. Sam Vaughn if she would take the presidency of the PBC ladies' auxiliary with Mrs. Maxwell as treasurer and get the group operating again. They agreed. Bess Vaughn became president June 12, 1930, and remained so through 1931. Hazel participated actively during these years, attending benefit teas and other fund-raising activities for PBC while her mother and her mother's friends served as officers. Mrs. Sam Vaughn was still president May 23, 1932, as the ladies council held another benefit tea. "Assisting in the dining room" was Mrs. Grover Leigh, chairman of the tea committee. Only seven women attended a couple of the women's council meetings in the fall and spring of 1932, and Hazel was not among them.[15]

A newspaper article in the *Fort Worth Press* in December 1932 noted that the PBC had reduced juvenile delinquency in Fort Worth by fifty percent in the six years since the club had been established.[16]

Bess Vaughn, after three years, still served as president in 1933 when the ladies sponsored an annual picnic for the boys at the "Boyville Gardens" Lake Worth site. Anne Burnett was still active, but by 1933 she was Mrs. James Goodwin Hall of New York.[17]

Ed A. Landreth, who was a member of the budget revision committee of the Community Chest, voiced an irony that few in Fort Worth would remember—but Hazel might have. In the spring of 1933 he predicted, "The two organizations will be merged in the long run." The budget revision committee had suggested that the YMCA and the Panther Boys' Club merge, but the latter was opposed. A half century later, mergers would be a major issue.[18]

Hazel was interested in the ladies' auxiliary work, but she read the newspaper avidly and kept up with society events. Her friend Ruth Googins met Elliott Roosevelt, the son of newly inaugurated Franklin D. Roosevelt, when Elliott visited the annual fat stock show in Fort Worth in the spring of 1933. It was a whirlwind courtship, for the two married in July that same year.[19]

The ladies' council remained small, with only eight members present at the fall, 1933, meeting when officers for the next year were elected. Mrs. Grover C. Leigh became first vice president. Technically, twenty-three ladies were cited as members.[20]

A month later Mrs. C. A. Lupton resigned as president of the ladies' council of the PBC, and the current first vice president, Hazel, took over and was later elected president. At their December meeting Hazel announced that Mrs. James Goodwin Hall would "again give the annual Christmas party for members of the Panther Boys' Club."[21]

Upon assuming the presidency, Hazel recognized that the ladies' group would need to increase in size to accomplish more for the club. Consequently,

Marie Lupton assisted Hazel from the earliest days. Shown with her a number of years later with her two daughters who also became active, Gloria Tennison (Mrs. Harry) and Shirley Geren (Mrs. Preston). Courtesy Fort Worth Public Library.

in January 1934, she launched a membership drive. Within only five months the membership "more than tripled." Part of the reason was that she inaugurated regular monthly meetings, instead of semi-annual ones, and planned lecture-type programs on general social service subjects, usually presented by a guest speaker.[22]

Hazel thus set out to inform herself and the ladies about the social needs of the boys of Fort Worth who could be helped by the Panther Boys' Club. Fort Worth had always been a charitable community, taking up funds to help its own. A consolidation of efforts began in 1907 called the Fort Worth United Charities, which by 1912 was renamed the Fort Worth Relief Association. The name Community Chest was adopted in 1923, making it the first Community Chest in the Southwest, but it disbanded in 1927 when it failed to raise its quota of funds. During this interim period when each agency was on its own, the Panther Boys' Club had been established. Then in 1929 the Chamber of Commerce, under the leadership of R. E. Harding, recreated the Community Chest with seventeen member agencies. (This organization would last until 1952 when it was reorganized as the United Fund and later the United Way.)[23]

About this time Hazel appeared in a group newspaper picture with twelve other women who were launching a campaign to inform Fort Worth women about the Community Chest. Each of the ladies chaired a committee in the Fort Worth Women's Crusade of the National Women's Committee Mobilization for Human Needs.[24]

Fort Worth, whose population reached 163,447 by 1930, was engaged in a large city building program, which delayed the impact of the Depression somewhat. However, the total number of permits awarded by the city for construction work on private homes fell from 1,998 in 1928 to 110 in 1934. People in the construction trades were thrown out of work.[25]

From 1930 on, the city canvassed neighborhoods to find jobs for the unemployed, and the welfare department urged working citizens to make needed home repairs and hire local people. Rotary Club members pledged to give the unemployed at least one day's work a month for the next three months. The Chamber of Commerce and the American Legion urged businesses to hire ten percent more people, to institute a six-hour workday, and to clean up, paint, and repair.[26]

The city welfare department helped as many as 2,000 people in several months in 1930. The Union Gospel Mission, the American Legion, the Salvation Army, the Community Chest, and even St. Joseph's Hospital handed out coffee and sandwiches to the needy. Mrs. Baird's Bakery donated day-old bread to the poor. And 1931 had the highest record ever of "gratuitous service" at City-County Hospital. Most people applying at the welfare department, however, wanted jobs, not charity.[27] Hazel and the ladies learned of the hundreds of men, women, and children living in tents, shacks, or single rooms of dilapidated rooming houses. Others slept on park benches, under bridges, and in doorways of buildings. Both city and county employees saw their salaries cut by twenty-five percent, and some began losing their jobs.[28]

At their ladies' auxiliary meetings Hazel and her friends mentioned stories of children collapsing at school from hunger. Newspaper articles reported that some students had to stay away from school because they had no shoes or stockings. The Kiwanis Club supplied these necessities to 175 youngsters.[29]

J. Frank Norris, whom Hazel remembered from her childhood, still preached at the First Baptist Church. Norris was organizing food donations and feeding sometimes 1200 people a week. Of the four most densely populated counties in Texas, Fort Worthians learned that the percentages of need were Tarrant, 25%; Bexar, 22%; Dallas, 19%; and Harris, 17%.[30]

Ladies at the June 1934 PBC Council meeting gave Hazel a vote of thanks for serving as president for the 1933–1934 club year and promptly re-elected her for a second term.

Knowing the conditions in their city and the need, Hazel led the ladies to numerous accomplishments in 1934. A "Women's Council Agenda" included repairs for the building, game room equipment (billiard tables, two sets of billiard balls, table games), library bookshelves, magazines, a dormitory or boys' home, selling the club to community, revising the men's and boys' supper, and a Halloween Party. The ladies planned teas and book reviews, at which admission would be charged to raise money to send the boys to camp. They contributed electrical equipment for the workshop and books for the library. They considered these projects in addition to emergency contributions of clothing and supplies so the boys could remain in school.[31]

They also began paying the tuition of a student at Texas Wesleyan College, for Mrs. Leigh reported to the ladies that he made two As and two Bs during his first semester. They also raised money for a cook stove for "Boyville Gardens." Sometimes the ladies planned no formal meeting but assembled at someone's home to mend shirts and darn socks for the boys. In December 1934, the clothing committee distributed about seventy-five items of clothing and shoes and fixed baskets of food for needy families. The director of the PBC wrote Mrs. Leigh a thank-you letter for all the work the ladies did in "gathering so much material for our repair work in the clubhouse." They had obtained paint and lumber.[32]

Hazel's first full calendar year as president of the PBC Council—1934—represented the ladies' busiest year to date. Membership tripled, and fund-raising activities for the club increased as well. Hazel's leadership and organizational abilities were emerging.

The director and men of the PBC appeared grateful for their efforts, so what could have happened to make Hazel and most of the ladies so unhappy that in January 1935 they withdrew their support and Hazel had no use for the PBC for the next fifty years? The answer created jealousy, rivalry, a determined Hazel, and a new boys' club.

CHAPTER 5

❦❦❦❦❦❦❦❦❦❦❦❦❦❦❦❦❦❦❦❦❦❦❦❦❦❦❦❦❦❦❦❦

The Ladies Split

At the Panther Boys' Club Ladies' Council meeting when things began to go wrong, Hazel was not even there. Her first vice president, Mrs. George W. Tinslar, presided as the women met in the library room of the PBC on June 11, 1934. Some of the ladies noticed that the library books they previously donated were missing. Mrs. Tinslar instructed Mrs. J. L. Rawley to investigate the whereabouts of the books and report at the next meeting.[1]

The PBC had been operating with Martha Justice as secretary and two college students directing activities. Alexander Campbell of the national organization, Boys' Clubs of America, Inc., met with Mrs. Vaughn and Mrs. Maxwell and said he was sending Mr. F. V. Thomson to become the PBC director. Thomson was past retirement age but was willing to work with the club; he began work August 1, 1934. In 1934 only four boys' clubs in Texas were affiliated with the national Boys' Clubs of America, Inc., organization: Panther Boys' Club in Fort Worth and clubs in El Paso, Waco, and Wichita Falls.[2]

Mr. Thomson, well educated in the boys' club movement, was professional and expected the PBC ladies' auxiliary only to raise funds. His attitude seemed to be that the BCA was a men's organization with the president of the ladies' auxiliary to be the only woman to serve on the administrative board of the boys' club. When the ladies understood Thomson's attitude, they did not like it.[3]

Apparently the ladies' club didn't meet over the summer; most such clubs operated September or October through May or June. At a specially called PBC Woman's Council board meeting in October at Hazel's home, Mrs. Rawley reported on the books missing from the library. They had been sold to Burford Salvage House at 215 Main Street. Cans of paint the women had donated were either missing or were found soiled. A month earlier, Bess Vaughn had attended a PBC board meeting at which they voted to hire a night watchman because things had been stolen from the club.[4]

Miss Martha Justice worked at the Panthers Boys' Club from 1926 to 1947. In 1934 Hazel and her ladies became upset with her and the PBC director. This photo was taken in 1940 when she was about thirty-two years old. Courtesy Wanda Gibson.

The women voted at their meeting not to place any more books in the library or spend any more money on the club until conditions improved. Meanwhile the ladies, in a letter dated October 29, 1934, requested that the new director check into the matter of the missing items. After all their efforts to provide materials for the boys or the club, the ladies did not appreciate their being sold for money. Surprisingly, their anger actually was directed against Martha Justice. She wasn't keeping a close enough eye on things, in their opinion.

Hazel wrote the letter of complaint for the ladies' council and addressed it to F. V. Thomson, Dr. Jack McLean, president of the board, and the PBC board of directors. The ladies decided not to "function as long as Miss Martha Justice is on the staff of the Panther Boys Club." Reasons they cited were:

(1) They donated money for books and found them stolen and sold to Burford Salvage House, 215 Main Street.

(2) Mrs. Lowden wanted to give $15 a month to a boy to attend school. Miss Justice chose one on her own. Mrs. Lowden checked to see if he was in school and found he wasn't, so she stopped sending money, but Miss Justice never called her or picked another boy.

(3) Miss Justice lost keys and allowed the paint to be stolen.

(4) When the ladies asked for a list of boys who needed shoes, Miss Justice neither investigated nor gave them a list.

(5) She failed to tell the ladies no Glee Club existed even when they advertised a tea saying that the Glee Club would sing at it.

(6) School supplies. [no explanation given]

(7) She showed favoritism toward boys.

(8) She showed lack of cooperation with the past three managers.

The ladies requested an immediate investigation before they gave any more money or supplies to the club. Possibly, Miss Justice saw her job as taking her orders from the PBC board and not from the ladies' auxiliary. The ladies were upset that she did not do their bidding.[5]

At the PBC board's regular meeting on Monday evening, November 12, 1934, "Mr. Bishop reported that the Special Committee appointed to inquire into the complaints of the Woman's Council against a member of the Staff had not yet met to consider the charges."[6]

Meanwhile, at their own November meeting Hazel read a letter from F. V. Thomson thanking the ladies "for their splendid efforts in gathering material for the repairs in the clubhouse." Because at least some of the paint he was thanking them for had been stolen and he didn't explain what happened, the ladies were not overjoyed by his letter.[7]

Three men from the PBC board of directors met December 6, 1934, and determined on their own to dismiss most of the charges the ladies made against Miss Justice. They did not call any of the ladies to ask their view of the facts. Four days later the entire men's board met and passed a resolution that "completely exonerates Miss Justice of and from said charges with certain minor exceptions." They mailed the report of the committee and the resolution to the ladies whose names and addresses they could obtain. The board also gave a unanimous vote of confidence to F. V. Thomson.[8]

Hazel and Thomson had not gotten along well since summer. He was new to town, so at his request she met with him and helped him find jobs for some of the boys and accompanied him to see the school superintendent. When they tried to get a boy into a vocational school, the superintendent said that a class could be formed if fifteen boys were interested. Hazel suggested that Miss Justice call the various principals of the schools and get the names of interested boys. It was the last she ever heard about the class.

"I made calls at the Club in an effort to cooperate with Mr. Thompson [sic] as he had said in the beginning if we would help him get the building remodeled so he could start his program, he would handle the situation concerning Miss Justice, insinuating he would have a man's [sic] club. It was my most earnest desire that things could be adjusted before our October meeting of the Woman's Council but I deeply regret that what I thought was cooperation has been so misjudged and it was never my intention to coerce or harass him as he implied at the board meeting. I am very sorry that the affairs of the Club are in this condition and I refer you to the two past managers of the Club as to their opinion of Woman's Council. All statements can be verified." Hazel added the last sentence in her own handwriting on a typed statement, which she sent to the men's board.[9]

Obviously, she and Thomson had a difference of opinion concerning how to work together. In a newspaper article that appeared years later Hazel told the reporter about the split. She said that board members told them that "they, not the women who raised the money, would decide how it should be spent."

"They told us: 'You've got to give your money to us. You all are just an auxiliary,'" Leigh said. "That made us mad."[10] The ladies were further angered when the PBC board gave Miss Justice a $10-per-month raise in salary at the same meeting that exonerated her.[11]

After the ladies got the letter from the board informing them of the decision at their meeting to exonerate Miss Justice and give Thomson a vote of confidence, they voted to change their name and take on a different project to assist needy boys. When the president of the board, Dr. McLean, called Hazel to try to patch up the dispute between the ladies and the PBC board, he assumed he could have some influence. After all, he was her medical doctor. She told him it was too late; the ladies had already decided.[12]

Personality problems between Hazel and Martha Justice or Hazel's "harassing" of Thomson and tendency to tell him and Miss Justice what to do may have caused some of the furor. What seemed to anger all the ladies, however, was that they raised the money, and things were missing. In addition, they did not like Thomson's attitude of "you ladies raise the money, but we men will decide how to spend it."

Martha Justice always believed that Hazel and the ladies became disillusioned with the executive director Thomson and left. That is what she told her husband, a boys' club director himself, when she married several years later. Even so, the two ladies (Hazel and Martha) did not speak at later Boys' Clubs of America, Inc., conventions, and it was common knowledge through the years that the two did not like each other.[13]

Hazel and the other ladies left PBC. They were playing bridge together one day shortly thereafter. Most of the ladies were active in the Woman's Club as well. Some of the ladies' husbands were friends or former business associates of Grover, and they had known each other in the oil business. They wanted to do something to help the unfortunate during the troubling times of the Depression. Bess Vaughn had been serving on the Works Progress Administration (WPA) board and mentioned to the ladies how much hunger existed on the North Side, the blue-collar part of the city with its packing houses and stockyards. Many of the families living there were first- or second-generation immigrants from central and eastern Europe.

Someone suggested that the ladies find a reading room or some other place where they could distribute children's clothes. Interest perked up around the card tables. Yes, that sounded like an outlet for their charitable efforts that would be appreciated. In a few days Hazel traveled to the North Side to take some clothing. Several of the society women were mothers of boys and so sent various sizes of boys' clothes.

"And at 410 NW Twenty-first Street the four Burklow boys lived, and they were playing in the street. I wanted them to go in the house to try on the clothes, but they couldn't because the house was locked.

"Why?" Hazel asked.

One of the boys explained that their mother worked at the packing house, and she was afraid four little boys in the house alone would burn the house down with their wood stove. The boys were in school in the daytime and played in front of the house or with their friends in the street for an hour or so until one of their parents came home from work.[14]

Hazel called a meeting of the ladies at her home on January 10, 1935, and explained the situation she had found to the eleven women. A report prepared

In a 1960 photo are four founding ladies with Hazel, seated on left. Mrs. Ed Lowden is seated center, and to her right is Mrs. C. A. Lupton. Standing are, left to right, Mrs. D. R. Tripplehorn and Mrs. B. F. Weekley. Courtesy Fort Worth Public Library.

by the juvenile department of the City of Fort Worth indicated that the North Side had the largest percentage of delinquency in the city. The North Side was the most populated area of Fort Worth with 32,573 in 1930 and 35,600 projected for 1939.[15]

When the boys had nowhere to go after school until their parents came home, it was no wonder they got in trouble. If they had a meeting place in the North Side, they might not become delinquent. Actually, a bus from PBC picked up boys in all areas of the city, including the North Side, and brought them to the club downtown at 600 East Weatherford; however, more boys would participate if they could walk to a place in their own neighborhood after school.

"If we just had a meeting place. . . ."

"We could take turns working one afternoon a week for an hour or two. We could organize a schedule."

Hazel apparently offered to organize everything if the ladies would volunteer to work. They rewrote the constitution from the women's council of the PBC to fit a new Fort Worth Boys' Club and adopted it unanimously.[16]

Shortly after that meeting, Hazel read in the newspaper that the Kiwanis Club of North Fort Worth had appointed an underprivileged children's chairman, Dr. Abe Greines who himself was second-generation, the son of an immigrant family who had arrived in North Fort Worth in 1905. His parents, Meyer and Sarah Greines, moved around a bit before coming to Fort Worth, and babies arrived periodically until finally there were five Greines boys and one girl. Abe, the third son, was born in Tyler, Texas, in 1896. The family later moved to Fort Worth. Abe graduated from North Side High School in 1914 and played football for TCU at the same time as Hazel's brother, Howard. Abe Greines was named an all-state tackle in 1916 and went on to obtain his medical degree at Baylor Medical School. A bachelor, Dr. Greines took part in numerous community activities and was a charter member of the Kiwanis Club of North Fort Worth.[17]

Boulevard Methodist Church, since torn down, stood at 1600 Boulevard in 1935 when the ladies obtained permission for the Fort Worth Boys Club to meet there. Mrs. Leigh later identified some of the boys in front as Jack King, Floyd Sargent, Luther Reagan, George Stancoff, Snooky Pressley, C. S. Minor, Knox Scott and O. L. Fuller. Courtesy Fort Worth Public Library.

Hazel and her mother went to Dr. Greines's office at 101 1/2 Northwest Twentieth to explain what the ladies wanted to do. Although Dr. Greines was intense, serious, and all business, he always had a smile on his face and was concerned about the less fortunate.[18]

"All the Greineses were alike; they never turned anybody down," a friend reminisced many years later.[19] Dr. Abe did not turn down Hazel and Bess either.

"I don't know what you mean by a boys' club, but if it's for boys, I'm willing to help." He suggested that they talk to Reverend L. L. Felder, pastor of the Boulevard Methodist Church at Northwest Fifteenth and Boulevard, to see about using their facility. Dr. Greines, who was Jewish, didn't attend that church, but the Greines family lived nearby at 1317 Circle Park Boulevard. Dr. Greines felt sure the Kiwanis Club of North Fort Worth would be willing to help. He invited Hazel and Bess to attend their luncheon the following Friday to explain the ladies' plans. Hazel accepted gladly and explained their proposed project.[20]

The men of the Kiwanis Club voted to provide utilities (about $5 per month), a building, and medical aid. Dr. Greines knew that he could furnish the medical assistance free. His friend and other tenant in his building, a dentist

Dr. Abe Greines, whose medical office was located across the street from the club, came over periodically to give free medical exams. Courtesy Fort Worth Public Library.

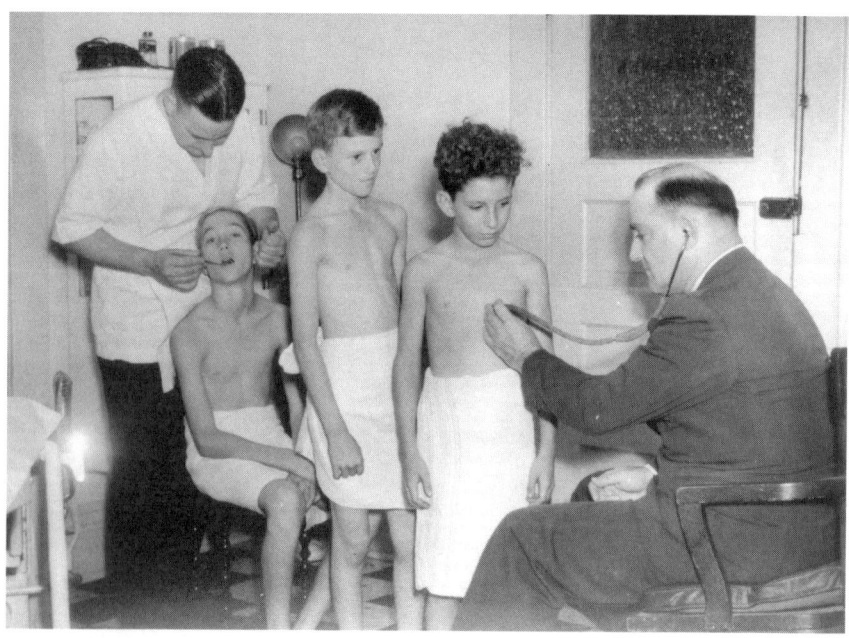

named Dr. Russell Calkins, could be counted on as well. Hazel volunteered her women to supervise the programs for the boys and to bear the remaining expenses. With this groundwork laid, Hazel called an executive committee meeting for January 24. Eleven members attended, and the treasurer reported $106.21 on hand.[21]

Hazel explained her activities since they had met two weeks earlier—her visit to see Dr. Greines, her speech to the Kiwanis' luncheon, her visit to the Reverend Felder. She also reported on a trip to Mr. Baker's office in the courthouse juvenile department of the City of Fort Worth. With him she had studied a map showing the need of a club in the North Side. He showed her that not only was North Fort Worth the area of greatest delinquency, but it had more boys per square block than any other section of the city. Hazel also had visited with the recreation supervisor for the city who suggested that the ladies should provide a library and assist the children with their homework each day.[22] Hazel had been busy.

Mrs. Ernest Allen moved to accept the offer of assistance from the men of the Kiwanis Club and to start a boys' club on the North Side. Mrs. Dominick Hart seconded the motion, and it carried. The ladies also voted to open on Friday, February 1, with an after-school party for the boys.

Hazel appointed Mrs. R. H. Kilpatrick as refreshment chairman and volunteered to contact the elementary schools in the area and invite the boys.[23] With the assistance of the city welfare department, Hazel visited three elementary schools—Denver Avenue, Circle Park, and Ellis Avenue. The principals allowed her to address the boys, and she asked if they would like a club. Some expressed some confusion about what would be involved.

"It would be a place to go and do anything they wanted to do," she told them, having in mind table tennis, checkers, basketball, etc.[24]

Friday afternoon, February 1, 1935, did not promise to be a good day for a beginning. The sky was dark; clouds hung low in the sky, and it had been raining off and on all day. About thirty-one women and five men from the Kiwanis Club assembled in the basement of the Boulevard Methodist Church. A newspaper reporter and a welfare worker or two came to see what would happen. Hazel and the ladies had baked cookies and were preparing hot chocolate, expecting about fifty boys. Mrs. A. A. Lund, wife of the manager of Armour and Company, arrived with a stack of books for the reading room.[25]

The hands on the clock showed 3:00 P.M., but nothing happened. Finally, at 3:15 a seven-year-old boy burst through the door and said, "They're coming." The principal of Denver Avenue Elementary was leading a line of boys as they walked the four blocks from the school to the church. The ladies learned that there were one hundred boys in the line. Soon boys were coming from every direction. They elbowed and fought each other to get in line for the hot chocolate.

Within a few minutes the ladies feared they would run out of hot chocolate, so they began watering it down; then it tasted scorched. They heard the boys commenting that it tasted funny.[26]

"This ain't no club, it's a church room," one boy yelled.

"Ain't we going to have any pool tables?"

"Shucks, they ain't got nothing here, not even a truck."

The ladies soon were busy settling disputes, ending fights. One boy told Mrs. Leigh, "You told us we could do anything we wanted to, and what we wanted to do was to whip the kid we couldn't whip at school."[27]

Of the 205 boys who showed up that first afternoon, Hazel always remembered seven-year-old Billy Burklow as the first child enrolled in the club, perhaps because he was the one who burst in and reported that everyone else was coming. One-fourth of the boys who came were Hispanic, and unfortunately, race problems existed in the area. North Main Street represented a dividing line between Anglos and Hispanics, with the Anglos mostly on the west and the Hispanics on the east. Some gang activity existed. Up until World War II fights generally ensued when youngsters of either ethnic group crossed the line and invaded the turf of the other.

The ladies didn't turn away the Mexican youngsters that first day, but Hazel called the director of Wesley Community House, a Methodist affiliate on Commerce Street east of North Main Street that worked with the Mexican boys. Arrangements were made for them to gather there after the social agency council of the Community Chest suggested it.[28]

Hazel admitted later that when she saw the first 100 boys crossing Boulevard, she "was frightened to death." The principal who had marched them over told her that the ladies and their efforts "wouldn't last a month. These boys will run you out."[29]

After it was all over, paper cups and napkins littered the yard of the Boulevard Methodist Church. The pastor told the ladies they couldn't use the facility anymore if the boys continued to litter like that and walk on the grass. The ladies wondered if they had taken on more than they could handle, and someone asked, "Whose idea was this?"[30]

Although many people cooperated then and through the years and although Dr. Greines the next year would become president of the new Fort Worth Boys' Club and Hazel secretary, few people ever doubted that this project was Hazel's baby. She was not shy in taking the credit, either. On the other hand, Dr. Greines, a busy family doctor, quiet and soft spoken, modestly took little of the credit. "It is Mrs. Leigh who was responsible for the organization," he always said.[31]

For Hazel, there was no turning back.

❦❦❦❦❦❦❦❦❦❦❦❦❦❦❦❦❦❦❦❦❦❦❦❦❦❦❦❦❦❦

CHAPTER 6

Fort Worth Boys' Club— A Life's Work

The ladies invited the boys to come back the next day—Saturday, February 2—to "their" club.

"Just don't walk on the grass," the Reverend Felder reminded. The day before, a photographer and *Fort Worth Star-Telegram* reporter had given the Friday opening events good publicity. Obviously, Hazel or someone called them in advance. Consequently, well over 100 boys showed up the next day at 9:00 A.M. Many of the society ladies could not return on Saturday, so only Hazel, her mother, and Mrs. Allen arrived. A young man named Fred Hanscom came from the city recreation department.[1]

Waiting outside before nine to keep the boys off the grass, were Hazel, Bess, and the Reverend Felder. The boys carefully stayed on the sidewalk. With no equipment or material for activities, it was hard to keep so many young men satisfied for very long.[2]

"We didn't know what to do with them," Hazel remembered later. She either called or had her mother call the New Isis Theatre and see if the owner, Mr. Louis Tidball, would treat the boys to a free movie as a charitable gesture. He would. They lined up the boys and marched several blocks to the movies. The Methodist Church gym was not available on Saturday afternoons, so the movie treat became a regular tradition those first weeks.[3]

"From the very beginning Mr. Tidball said that anytime I'd call him, he would let me bring the boys. Later he worked it out to give so many passes, and a boy had to mow the yard to get that nickel pass." Hazel learned not to be shy in asking for free materials, donated services, volunteered time, or money for the boys.[4]

Meanwhile the ladies, many of whom were not shy either, rounded up sports equipment and other materials. Mrs. F. J. Adams collected a host of boys' books and magazines, and Mrs. Lund sent bookshelves. Within a week they had a library of 150 books. It can be reasonably assumed that a close watch was kept on things, and the books and equipment did not disappear to be resold at a salvage shop.[5]

Shortly after organizing the club, making up a membership list, and getting membership cards for the boys, Hazel and the ladies, as well as the North Fort Worth Kiwanis men, supported the use of "The Boys' Club Code" as adopted by the BCA national headquarters. At every opportunity they had the boys reciting in unison:

"I believe in God and the right to worship according to my own faith and religion.

I believe in America and the American way of life, in the Constitution and the Bill of Rights.

I believe in fair play, honesty and sportsmanship.

I believe in my Boys' Club which stands for these things."[6]

During that first spring the club was open from 3:00 to 6:00 P.M. on school days and from 9:00 A.M. to 1:00 or 2:00 P.M. on Saturdays for boys ages six to fourteen.[7]

Quickly the ladies created a new organization called the Fort Worth Boys' Club. When they met February 11, they cited the 205 boys they enrolled that first day, reported $113.71 in the treasury, and voted to pay a Mr. George Harrington $15 per month to assist at the club. Within less than two weeks they had enrolled over 300 boys. The ladies also agreed to save the comics out of their own newspapers for the boys, because they knew that most of the boys' families could not afford to subscribe.[8]

In those first few weeks of operation two boys fainted at the club. Hazel put them in her car and took them to Dr. Greines's office a few blocks away. "This is nothing but malnutrition," he said.[9]

Hazel immediately reported this to the other ladies; someone repeated the story at a Junior League meeting, and Mrs. J. Lee Johnson, Jr., wrote a check for $600 to buy food for the boys. The club then began serving snacks when the boys arrived from school.[10]

The ladies planned an Easter-egg hunt to be held in Marine Park, near the corner of Twentieth and North Main, a few blocks north of the Boulevard Methodist Church. The ladies planned hot dogs, Coca Cola, and cakes—occasionally Mrs. Baird's Bakery would donate day-old cakes. The ladies met earlier to dye the eggs. Actually, on the day of the egg hunt it rained, and they transferred the party to the basement of the church, but little boys' spirits were hard to dampen. During "National Youth Week," the last week in April, Mrs. Allen conducted a program on citizenship, and Mrs. Ed Lowden took the boys on a tour of her husband's business, Stafford-Lowden Company. A show window of Monnig's Department Store downtown displayed handicrafts made by the boys.[11]

When the ladies elected new officers, Hazel became president of what was already being called the Fort Worth Boys' Club. They also considered themselves the women's council for the club.[12]

During the summer, activities continued with two Texas Christian University students working as physical director and assistant. They took the boys on hikes and on a series of industrial tours visiting factories in the area. In July Mrs. Leigh volunteered the boys to publicize the club by doing programs for the Botanic Garden Center. On July 8, 1935, the State of Texas issued a charter to the Fort Worth Boys' Club.[13]

The Kiwanis continued to help, and Mr. J. E. Mills gave a watermelon party for the boys on the lawn of the Texas Electric Service Company plant near Paddock Viaduct. Roy Queen sang cowboy songs and performed tricks with his horse. From the 100 boys who attended, Dr. Greines received one patient.[14] One person got hurt at the event.

In September they decided to begin a membership drive for the ladies' club that would end in January 1936. Hazel divided the existing membership of about thirty women into three groups. The other two groups would entertain the group that signed up the most new members or collected the most dues from old members. In addition, the ladies made application to be an agency of the Community Chest.[15]

The ladies provided clothing for fifty boys so they could start school in September. Additional donated items for the club included a Victrola, games, curtains, four chairs and a table, and a rug. They were having covered dish luncheons and morning "coffees" to attract new members to their own group.[16]

The Ladies Fort Worth Boys' Club Council held teas and socials routinely and drew large membership including L to R Mrs. C. C. Westfall, standing; Mrs. Clyde Carter, seated; Mrs. Buddy Markum, next to Hazel, standing right. Courtesy Fort Worth Public Library.

By October the boys' club attendance boasted 627 boys enrolled, a total monthly attendance of 1,654, with an average daily attendance of sixty-one. The only person on full pay at the club was Mr. Dunlap at $5 a week[17]

The boys repeated the pledge of allegiance and sang "America" at a patriotic memorial program on Friday afternoon November 22 to honor Will Rogers, who had died in an airplane crash in Alaska. The Worth post of World War Nurses presented a flag to Mrs. Leigh and Dr. Greines, which was raised on the flagpole and then lowered to half mast. Major O. E. Paxton, Jr., commandant of cadets at North Side High School and J. P. Elder Junior High, explained the meaning of the flag and the care and display of it. They took a collection for the Will Rogers Memorial Fund, and boys were able to donate money they earned at the club by raking leaves and cleaning the building.[18]

Hazel and the ladies took an interest in specific boys who showed talent. In November, Mrs. C. C. Patterson, chairman of the music activities, secured a teacher to give individual accordion lessons for a youngster named Johnny Kohut. Another boy, Otis Snow, whose father was a disabled veteran from

World War I, was encouraged to join the first Glee Club. They found an art teacher to give lessons to a boy who showed promise in art.[19]

The ladies secured a location at 511 Houston Street downtown for a white-elephant sale, an indoor and 1930s version of what later generations would call a garage sale, yard sale, or flea market. They planned their fund raiser for December 5, 6, and 7. The membership drive had resulted in over one hundred additions to the ladies group, so most pitched in to make the sale a success. They created committees on cakes and candy, fruits and nuts, jellies and jams, furniture and toys, with a dozen women or so on each committee. There were also committees for publicity, cashiers, etc. One committee even furnished musical entertainment each afternoon of the sale. The ladies served a luncheon each of the three days to draw businessmen and others. Mrs. Morgan Bryan was in charge of the entire event.

The music committee proudly invited the Boys' Glee Club from the FWBC to sing. There were accordion numbers too, so that Johnny Kohut was able to show what he had been learning from his lessons.[20]

In that Depression year of 1935 the ladies made $225, with a few more pledges to come in later. Indeed, the Junior League made "a most generous donation of $400" for emergencies at the club.[21]

Even though the society ladies and the Kiwanis Club of North Fort Worth were working hard for the boys, needy girls were not being ignored in Fort Worth either. The Girls' Service League, an organization formed during World War I to help single young women who might need assistance, held a marketing show all week the same week as the FWBC ladies held their white-elephant sale. The Girls' Service League ladies served dinners and luncheons and raised $975 for the upkeep of their two homes for needy girls, Lassiter Lodge and Worth Cottage.[22]

Hazel's brother Howard helped a lot at the club, as did his wife, Mickey, who made apple pie and brought it to the football players. Grover apparently did not come to the club enough to be noticed by the boys. Several of the "regulars" among the boys commented later that they never knew that "Miz" Leigh had a husband. In their unconcerned state they didn't pay any attention if she was a "Miss," married, or a widow. Grover was then working long hours as a deputy sheriff or deputy marshal. Hazel later told an interviewer, however, that her husband was interested in the boys and proud of the club.[23]

Congress passed the Emergency Relief Appropriation Act in 1935 and made available nearly $5 billion for relief nationwide. Created that year were the Works Progress Administration (WPA) and the National Youth Administration (NYA), which was a sort of junior WPA. The main purpose of the latter agency was to provide part-time employment for high school and college students age sixteen through twenty-five. Hazel applied for NYA workers but did not find them all reliable. She had to train them to work in the office or the game room. She needed someone at the door to make sure every boy signed in every day. She wanted to keep good records, but she also wanted to make sure that only boys who were members came to the club. When each boy had joined, he filled out his parents' names and address so they could be reached if necessary.[24]

The PBC had always given a big Christmas party for the boys, so, of course, this would have to be done for the boys of the Fort Worth Boys' Club. Saturday, December 21, 1935, would be the date. Mrs. H. B. Simcox served as chairman of the party. The ladies worked hard for several days before the event, soliciting donations, buying the rest, and preparing stockings with fruit, nuts, and candy for three hundred boys. Unfortunately, it poured down rain that day, so only 154 showed up. The ladies kept track of who came and who did not—the value of the sign-in again—and handed out stockings early the next week to the "regulars" who had missed the party.

At the party Reverend Felder told the Christmas story. Dr. Greines apparently didn't mind being ecumenical about it all, for he participated in the party and distributed the stockings.[25] At the January, 1936, board meeting Mrs. Simcox reported on expenses for the Christmas party: candy, $5; nuts, $9.15; oranges, $1; apples, $2.73; stockings, $4; popcorn balls, $2; for a total of $23.88.[26]

Members of the Kiwanis Club always supported the ladies in major activities, and the club was a joint effort between them. Things did not always go smoothly, however, for the men volunteers wanted the major activities to be sports and pool, while the society ladies wanted to teach the younger boys table manners, proper dress, and posture. "We used to take our lace tablecloths from home and our silver and candelabras."[27] Hygiene was high on their list, as well. Hazel remembered that on the first day the "smell of those little boys was simply overpowering and it nauseated one of my ladies."[28]

The ladies started out maintaining rules and discipline. This issue was another that had bothered them at the PBC, because for a time only a couple of college students and the youthful secretary Martha Justice had been in charge. At the FWBC, if a boy caused trouble he had to sit behind a door, write his name repeatedly, or even leave and go home. "No, no, no, no, no, no," Mrs. Leigh would say to a boy doing something wrong.[29] "If you do right by a child," Hazel maintained, "he doesn't resent being corrected."[30]

Keeping the boys busy became part of the strategy. The club couldn't afford to hire a janitor, so they organized the boys to care for the building, the grounds, and the equipment. Many paid their dues by working for the club.[31]

As the ladies summed up their accomplishments for the first year, they reviewed that they had helped more than 100 boys with 427 articles of clothing. One member made a contribution of new shoes for fifteen boys, and five additional pairs were distributed as well. Dr. Greines supplied emergency medical aid to 40 boys, and six boys received new glasses. During the year 654 different boys attended a total of 18,167 times. They listened to twenty lectures on first aid, hobbies, good citizenship, and the Bible. Musical instruction was

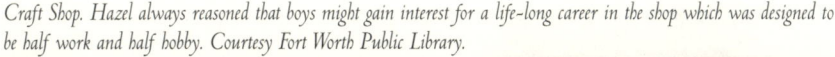

Craft Shop. Hazel always reasoned that boys might gain interest for a life-long career in the shop which was designed to be half work and half hobby. Courtesy Fort Worth Public Library.

given to all members. Best of all, the juvenile department of the City of Fort Worth reported that delinquency had been reduced by seventy-five percent in the North Side that year.[32]

Various ladies or clubs volunteered to plan activities for one afternoon a week—the Junior League took Wednesdays. Hazel was there every afternoon, however. Besides their numerous volunteer hours at the Fort Worth Boys' Club, the ladies' group held book reviews, bridge tournaments, luncheons, and teas at members' homes for which they charged an admission fee in order to raise money for the club. At one tea the admission was a bath towel and soap. The ladies collected 290 towels and 372 bars of soap for the boys, plus $10 cash.[33]

At another tea Mrs. Lupton displayed souvenirs from her trip to Australia; the Boys' Glee Club sang, and Johnny Kohut played the accordion. Hazel put her telephone number in the paper asking for the donation of an accordion for him. She took Johnny with her to radio station KTAT on Wednesday, October 9, to play selections as she made a pitch for the club.[34]

Bess Vaughn protested to Hazel that she really didn't want her to get as involved as she did. Hazel was at the club every day as the voluntary executive director. "She thought it was too dangerous for me to be out there on the North Side," Hazel explained.[35]

By the end of that first year four male employees were on duty each day. The athletic director, Bill Hudson, organized three softball teams to play four games a week for eight weeks. Their names were the Frogs, the Steers, and the Bears. A later team, in honor of Dr. Greines, called themselves the "Pill Rollers."[36]

CHAPTER 7

⚜⚜⚜⚜⚜⚜⚜⚜⚜⚜⚜⚜⚜⚜⚜⚜⚜⚜⚜⚜⚜⚜⚜⚜⚜⚜⚜⚜⚜⚜⚜⚜

A Building of Their Own

*A*ctivities for the FWBC did not take all the time in the daily life of Hazel Vaughn Leigh. She won an appointment to the Texas Centennial Livestock and Frontier Days Exposition Commission. Texas was celebrating its one-hundredth birthday, and Fort Worth wanted its celebration to be worthy of the Lone Star State.[1]

Fort Worth had applied for and received a portion of the $3 million in state funds set aside by the legislature for the festivities. Councilman William N. Monnig, Sr., president of the exposition board, had only announced the appointments six days before the meeting. The 200 women named to the board included Mrs. Marvin Leonard, Mrs. H. C. Meacham, Mrs. Elliott Roosevelt (whom Hazel had known years before as Ruth Googins), Mrs. Winfield Scott, Mrs. W. C. Stripling, and Mrs. Dave Tandy. Two hundred men were also invited to serve on the board."[2]

Dedication ceremonies for the Frontier Centennial, which featured Casa Mañana, a Billy Rose–produced show, and Sally Rand and her dancers, were July 18. The show officially opened at 3:30 P.M. that day when President Franklin D. Roosevelt, while fishing on his yacht off the coast of Maine, pushed a button which sent an electrical impulse that cut a lariat in Fort Worth. The lariat fell and festivities began. That's what you could do when the president's daughter-in-law, Ruth Googins Roosevelt, served on the committee.[3]

Another activity of Hazel's: Grover remained a deputy U.S. marshal in 1936, and sometime during that year Hazel either traveled with him or was employed individually by the U.S. government to help transport two narcotics patients to Alderson, West Virginia. The U.S. marshal's department apparently needed a woman to help transport women. Hazel jumped at the chance to travel.[4] Unfortunately, newspaper articles, minutes of board meetings, and other methods of documenting events do not record her non–boys' club activities thoroughly. But the FWBC remained her primary occupation.

Each year in January, the boys who were members of the club received new membership cards. One had to be a member to attend the club and to take part in games and activities. Each boy had to pay $1 a year to make the membership have more value to him, but boys who could not afford the $1 dues could easily work out their payment.

The Kiwanis Club of North Fort Worth hosted a turkey dinner on Tuesday evening, January 14, 1936, at the Boulevard Methodist Church facility for the 200 boys who had the best attendance for the previous year. Bess Vaughn served as banquet chairman, so, of course, the ladies and Kiwanis were doing it together; the Kiwanis helped physically and paid for the meal.[5]

After almost a year as an active club, things should have been running smoothly, the boys settled down and behaved well, accustomed to the routine and the behavior expected of them. If the ladies had forgotten that the North Side was the rough part of town, the most populated section, the thickest concentration of blue-collar working-class families, they soon got a reminder. These boys were the kind who roamed the streets knocking out street lights, threw rocks at the "colored" kids, and stole nickels out from under the empty milk bottles on people's doorsteps.

The 200 youngsters who won their places at the turkey dinner by good attendance marched into the church basement for dinner that Tuesday evening in perfect control. A Kiwanis man sat at each table with a group of boys, but the men were busy visiting with each other when the ladies started serving and so neglected to pay attention.

After the boys finished eating, they threw things, even plates, at each other, and pandemonium erupted in the church basement. The hosts' and hostesses' first thoughts were that they would be criticized for not keeping better order. Hazel raised her voice and yelled, "If you don't quiet down, we'll close the club tomorrow!" Silence fell over the room. The boys sat quietly for ten minutes before they filed out with shamed looks.[6]

"All that we had been working for seemed to crumple under us, and the next few months found our own sponsors most difficult to hold together," Hazel remembered later. She thought better facilities with more space for activities geared to the boys would help.[7]

At the March meeting of the ladies' group, Mrs. Bert Weekley made a motion "that we unite with the North Side Kiwanis in an effort to raise funds

Mr. and Mrs. Bert Weekley, left, and Mr. and Mrs. George Scaling. Courtesy Fort Worth Public Library.

to erect a building for the boys on the North Side." As soon as the motion passed and they began working toward that aim, the ladies put aside money for a building fund. By July 1, they had raised $1,500, no small feat during the Depression.[8]

In a semi-annual report covering the first six months of 1936, the ladies reported nineteen citizenship lectures given, three health lectures, as well as twenty-four picture shows. (Generous Mr. Tidball at the New Isis Theatre was not imposed upon totally. The staff workers took the boys to movies at the Liberty and the Rose Theatres as well.) The Boulevard Methodist Church gymnasium still was not available on Saturday afternoons. Signed up to construct things in the workshop were 100 boys, fifty in the Glee Club, twenty-five in a rhythm band, six in guitar class, and twenty-five boys in a commercial art class.[9]

Because Community Chest funds had not yet been approved, the husband of one of the member ladies paid the salary for the athletic director to work three hours a day. Several ladies who volunteered were wives of oil company personnel whom Grover had known back in the 1920s at Marland Oil. As independent oil entrepreneurs, several of them had become quite wealthy.

Meatpacking executives from the stockyards and other businessmen supported the club, mainly because their wives had become interested through their social and charitable club activities.

At the September meeting, the ladies appointed three women to go with three Kiwanis Club men to visit the Community Chest "to find out what distribution is to be made of Community Chest funds allotted to Boys Clubs." This would not be the last time that Hazel would plunge in and do something and then ask for Community Chest or United Fund help after the fact. The charitable organizations proved more amenable when they had been involved in the planning process, as Hazel would later learn.[10]

In 1938 the ladies gave credit to A. A. Lund for influencing the Community Chest to release funds for the boys' club. Hazel was learning that as long as one had important and influential friends, many doors would open.[11]

Across the city, the Centennial celebration continued in full swing with famous people in town as a part of the show. When dancer Sally Rand promised to attend a morning coffee and style show sponsored by the boys' club ladies at the home of Mrs. Gladys Westbrook on September 30, approximately 400 women attended. That Johnny Kohut was also playing his accordion was probably not the real attraction. He enjoyed missing school and eating the buffet of tiny link sausages, midget biscuits, and preserves anyway.[12]

Official organization prior to constructing a building for the boys came in mid-October 1936. Four men and three women met and decided to call the club the Fort Worth Boys' Club, Inc. For a six-person board they chose three members from the North Fort Worth Kiwanis and three from the ladies' group. Each group was then to select five more members to create a sixteen-member board of directors. The smaller board worked so well for them that the sixteen-member board of directors met infrequently, sometimes annually, if they met at all. At a specially called meeting the following day, the ladies' club ratified what had been done the day before. Officers of the FWBC, Inc., were Dr. Abe Greines, president; Green B. Trimble, vice president; Mrs. Grover Leigh, secretary; and J. E. Mills, treasurer. They placed an option on a lot for a building at the same meeting in which they organized and elected officers.[13] Formal state application for incorporation was made on October 31, 1936, listing the six board members of the FWBC, Inc., as Dr. Abe Greines, Green B. Trimble, J. E. Mills, Mrs. Grover C. Leigh, Mrs. Bert Weekley, and Mrs. J. C.

Maxwell.[14] The three men also were members of the committee on the under-privileged of the Kiwanis Club of North Fort Worth, with Dr. Greines as chairman. Other men on the underprivileged committee were W. C. Miller and Judge Tom Renfro.

Later that month the ladies amended their constitution and added the word "council" to it. Their club thus became the Fort Worth Boys' Club Council. With a membership of 130 ladies in the council and twenty-five prominent businessmen in the Kiwanis Club, the FWBC had enough support, needed since the average daily attendance of boys at the club reached eighty-four by November with 814 members registered.[15]

Someone with a connection at Western Olds [Oldsmobile] Company suggested a promotion to raise money for the club. The dealership agreed to donate twenty cents to the FWBC building fund for each visitor to their showroom who looked at the new models and signed the guest book—one per family, sixteen or older. The promotion would run Saturday, Sunday, and Monday, November 14–16. If 1,000 people stopped by, looked at the cars, and registered, the club would raise $200. Hostesses from the council poured coffee from 2:30 to 5:00 P.M. each afternoon. Western Olds turned over $100 to the ladies at the end of the promotion, so 500 registered.[16]

The newspapers reported the activities of the Fort Worth Boys' Club and news of the Panther Boys' Club as well. If Hazel's blood pressure could be influenced by what she read, it would have soared as she saw accounts of Panther Boys' Club activities while she was clipping stories for her scrapbook about the North Side efforts. The Panther Club was celebrating its tenth anniversary in 1936, and articles publicized their activities the very weekend of the Western Olds' promotion. The Panther Club membership had grown from 783 to 1,306 during their tenth anniversary year.[17] "Over 1,000 books were circulated from the library." Hazel would have fumed when she read that, remembering the books she and her friends had donated or purchased that were sold at the second-hand store.[18]

Most of the ladies on the Panther Boys' Club Ladies' Council, of which Hazel had been president when the women left the PBC, now supported the FWBC. Not all had abandoned the PBC, however. One who did not was Anne Burnett, the former Mrs. Guy Waggoner, by 1936 Mrs. James Goodwin Hall. For many years she would host the annual Panther Boys' Club Christmas party.

While the club met at Boulevard Methodist Church, the boys played football and other sports in the park, or boulevard, in front of the church. Physical education coach Corky Makarwich is standing at left. Courtesy Fort Worth Public Library.

Local and out-of-town celebrities dropped by the North Side Club when anyone had a contact to bring them there. Sam Baugh, TCU's All-American football player, came in 1936 treating the boys to a passing exhibition one Friday afternoon in December. The new athletic director, C. C. "Corky" Makarwich, who began work that month, persuaded Baugh to come and bring Kyle Aldrich. The two TCU football players played touch football with the boys. Baugh's team was the "skins" and Aldrich's, the "shirts"; Corky refereed.[19]

Corky Makarwich would provide stability as the athletic director. Having grown up on the North Side at 2100 Lee, Corky worked at Harvey Ice Cream company at Twenty-first and Commerce for seven years after grade school. He learned Mrs. Leigh's technique of asking for free merchandise "for the boys" and persuaded his former boss to donate ice cream. Harvey also sold milk, and with the bottle cap from a bottle of Harvey's milk, the boys could get in free at the New Isis Theatre.[20]

Corky certainly walked the boys to the theatre frequently. On one occasion he took them there to view the car in which Bonnie Parker and Clyde Barrow were killed in a shoot-out with law enforcement officers in Louisiana. The theatre had arranged to exhibit it. Corky told the boys, "Now this is what happens to you when you turn to crime." Makarwich, in fact, broke up a gang of boys in the area who called themselves the "Dirty Dozen." The boys were collecting junk scrap iron to sell to a junk man who then sold it to Japan. Corky caught the boys stealing the iron from the local man and then selling it back to him. The boys were members of the club at the time. He simply let them know that he knew and gave them a severe reprimand. One of the boys later commented that Mrs. Leigh relied on Corky to keep them in line. "We were rambunctious."[21]

At the Methodist Church boys sometimes threw things from the mezzanine, where the shop was located, to the gym and then hid in the woodshop. They remembered Makarwich as a strict disciplinarian but respectfully called him "Mr. Mac."[22]

Dr. Greines had persuaded Corky to take the job as athletic director, and he did it under protest. "I agreed to try it for thirty days. I took the boys outside to the island of the boulevard for football and then played basketball in the Boulevard Methodist Church gym." Corky refereed or umpired whichever was necessary. Dr. Greines, always worried that the boys were not getting enough to eat, would give Corky cod liver oil pills and vitamins for the boys. Corky

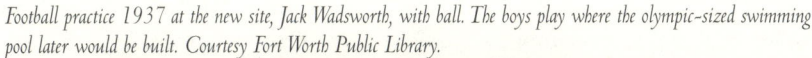

Football practice 1937 at the new site, Jack Wadsworth, with ball. The boys play where the olympic-sized swimming pool later would be built. Courtesy Fort Worth Public Library.

taught the boys first aid, how to keep a batting average, how to keep basketball scores, etc. The job worked out so well for him that he stayed for five years. He attended TCU in the mornings and was at the boys' club in the afternoons. Later, he taught shop at Castleberry and Trimble Tech and then went into the construction business. He officiated at high school and college football games for thirty-five years.[23]

Mrs. Leigh apparently did not hold it against Makarwich that he had been a member of Panther Boys' Club as a youngster. After all, there was no FWBC at the time.

One of the youngsters Corky worked with was Snooky Pressley, who was a whiz at baseball. "I would pitch to Snooky and he would hit it out of the park behind the building every time; he was a natural for professional baseball."[24] Snooky, one of the youngsters who joined the club the first year or so at about age nine, lived at 1703 Boulevard, only a block from the Methodist Church where the club first met. In 1936 he was the FWBC marble champ in a countywide contest sponsored by the *Fort Worth Press*. Filled with energy, he often was sent to the back of the line for squeezing in and being generally mischievous. Julian "Snooky" Pressley later explained, "Everybody was really poor, no bicycles, no money. A lot of the boys would have gone to the pen if it hadn't been for the boys' club." Snooky's activities at the club were curtailed when he took a *Fort Worth Star-Telegram* paper route, which he held for several years.[25]

"Snooky had a lot of character," one of the other boys remembered years later.[26]

Alexander Campbell of the Boys' Clubs of America, Inc., visited Fort Worth and drew up plans for a new building. His plans would cost $50,000 to implement; the ladies and the Kiwanis knew they could not afford that. Mr. Campbell told them that the most reasonably constructed boys' club he knew about was one in Alexander, West Virginia, which had cost $25,000. That was too much, as well. When Mr. Campbell saw that the Fort Worth Boys' Club supporters did not have much money, he did not think they were serious about a building. "When you are ready to build, let me know," he told them.[27]

The ladies and men were ready; they just lacked money. They forged ahead anyway. They agreed that the Kiwanis would select a site and obtain it. In the meantime, the ladies would secure an architect and plan the building. Architect Robert P. Woltz, Jr., drew up plans for the building, which would include a

40' x 72' gymnasium, a game room, a library, workshop, showers, locker room, and kitchen. This version, 98' x 60' in all, would cost $16,000 to complete.[28]

By late October 1936, the men had purchased a lot at the corner of Northwest Twentieth and Ellis Avenue, the site of the old B. W. Owens Lumber Company shed. The boys' club board authorized Dr. Greines to obtain a federal loan, but he was unable to do so; thus each club decided to seek personal loans. Each club, the men Kiwanis and the ladies Council, decided to raise $2,500 to get started on the building. Mrs. Weekley signed a note guaranteeing the amount the ladies needed, and the Kiwanis did the same. Thus together they borrowed $5,000 from the First National Bank for three months. At the end of that time they renewed the loan with a mortgage on the building.[29]

Hazel, Mrs. Weekley, and Green B. Trimble sought the aid of Trav Lewis of organized labor to donate services to construct the building. The three presented their plans to various local union presidents at a dinner December 28, 1936, at the vocational school. George Scaling and Mrs. Ross Trimble were also present.[30]

As a result, when work started with the groundbreaking April 10, 1937, members of the Fort Worth Bricklayers' Union donated time to build the new red-brick structure. Boys came from Boulevard Methodist Church to help carry bricks. Also donating their time and labor were the carpenters, plumbers, and electricians unions. A modified Spanish-style architecture prevailed.[31]

From their combined funds, the two sponsoring organizations paid a supervisor $250 per month until their money ran out in July 1937. Hazel was on the site everyday, and Dr. Greines's office was located across Northwest Twentieth Street, so calls could be made to ask for building materials donations and to check on the volunteer labor. The outside of the building was complete by mid-summer.[32]

Even though the building was incomplete, in July the ladies and Kiwanis decided to hold a dedication ceremony. It would inform participants of progress and be an opportunity to get publicity in the newspapers; donations might follow. After a luncheon meeting of the Kiwanis at Boulevard Methodist Church on July 2, attendees got in their cars and drove north the few blocks to the Northwest Twentieth and Ellis site. Judge Walter Morris acted as master of ceremonies, and Sidney Samuels spoke as a dedication plaque was unveiled.

The Fort Worth Boys Club moved into its new building at 100 Northwest Twentieth Street in September 1937. Courtesy Fort Worth Public Library.

Meanwhile, inside finishing touches continued, and the board requested an $8,070 annual budget from the Community Chest.[33]

On moving day—September 10, 1937—the boys helped move from the temporary rented quarters to the new building. Ice cream and cake, toys and balloons, and short speeches made opening day an occasion.[34]

The Fort Worth recreation department band presented a concert as the first program in the new building. The adults could not resist making a few short speeches because of the pride they felt in their accomplishment. The president of the Kiwanis Club of North Fort Worth, Ross Trimble, spoke, as did Dr. Abe Greines and Hazel, FWBC board secretary and president of the Fort Worth Boys' Club Council. Hazel always liked to remind everyone that the building was the first building in Texas to be constructed solely as boys' club. Even the Panther Boys' Club still operated in rented facilities downtown.[35] Also on the day the new building opened, Mrs. Dominick Hart, II, librarian for the club, brought 100 volumes of Tom Swift books that her own three sons had outgrown. Fall projects for the boys would include finishing touches (such as painting or varnishing) to the building, cleaning up leftover construction debris, and working on the playgrounds.[36]

Other events of 1937 seemed minor compared to the completion of their new building, but important things occurred. In April the Glee Club was invited to sing in San Antonio at the convention of the Texas Federation of Music Clubs. The WPA agreed to pay some workers, and the board voted in November 1937 to hire Hazel as executive director at $100 per month as soon as the Community Chest funds were available. Corky Makarwich was to be paid $100 as activities director. The money still had not been approved, however.[37]

A report for the year's activities appeared in the newspaper at the end of 1937. These activities were typical for the club during this time: fourteen musical programs, five health lectures, twenty-three citizenship lectures, one trip to the zoo, one trip to the stock show, one minstrel show, baseball, and movies. There were five wiener roasts, snacks and milk, lunch twenty-six times, turkey dinner for 200, Christmas party for 300, and baskets of food and nuts were sent to seventy-one families. Also there were 824 pieces of clothing given, sixty pairs of shoes, 600 homes visited, and sewing classes for mothers. Total membership of the club was 830.[38]

The FWBC had its building, but it wasn't paid for, and fund-raising activities continued. Eighty prominent businessmen in Fort Worth presented an all-men's show in February. The ladies' council collected recipes for an eighty-page cookbook to sell. Recipes for "Mayonnaise Chicken" and "Burnt Almond Parfait" were attributed to Mrs. Grover Leigh, and the ladies dedicated the book to Hazel. Mrs. Franklin Delano Roosevelt submitted a recipe for "White House Scrambled Eggs." President and Mrs. Roosevelt's son Elliott was then living in Fort Worth with his wife.[39]

Fifty-one different National Youth Administration boys and girls worked at the club during the year. They earned a small wage paid by the government while being trained as librarians, clerical workers, supervisors, etc. As they became more competent they were helped to find other employment. One young lady wanted to be a nurse but could not save enough money. One of the ladies helped her out financially, and she began her college studies. Hazel had to fill out a long form on each NYA worker. They would barely get trained enough to be of help and then would move on to better jobs, and a new group would come in. Other workers in the North Side, at the stockyards, were earning from $0.30 to $0.36 per hour.[40]

The Fort Worth Boys' Club finally appeared in the 1938 "Parade of Community Chest Agencies," a six-page pamphlet. Their budget shown by the Community Chest was $9,500, so things were looking up. The FWBC board approved $15 car expenses for Hazel (who was by then signing her name Mrs. Hazel Leigh instead of Mrs. Grover Leigh) and purchased a used pick-up truck.[41]

A newspaper clipping indicated that Mr. and Mrs. Sam Vaughn attended an Old Settlers Reunion at Everman on Sunday, May 1, 1938. Apparently Hazel and Grover did not go—further indication that their lives were going in different directions. Grover made at least one serious attempt, however, to create a life for them together. He rented an apartment at 2744 Willing and persuaded Hazel to move there with him. Within months she was back at 1941 Forest Park Boulevard with her parents, and Grover stayed at the Willing address.[42]

Their marriage was falling apart.

CHAPTER 8

✤✤✤✤✤✤✤✤✤✤✤✤✤✤✤✤✤✤✤✤✤✤✤✤✤✤✤✤✤✤✤✤✤

Wartime Worries

In the 1940s many of the young boys who started out in the FWBC during the first two or three years were old enough to go away to war—and die. Later there would be even more family heartbreak for Hazel. Of "her" boys, Snooky Pressley would go; so would Otis Snow, and little Billy Burklow.

When World War II began in Europe in September 1939, President Franklin D. Roosevelt realized early on that the United States needed to be ready. Preparation and training for the probable U.S. entrance resulted in the old World War I airfield on the North Side, Taliaferro, being reopened as Hicks Field for pilot training. Hazel wondered if the old Barron Field near the Vaughns' land in Everman would reopen too.[1]

Work at the boys' club kept Hazel busy. Besides being the secretary of the FWBC board, she continued to serve as president of the ladies council and worked at the new club as full time executive director.

Indebtedness on the building and equipment had been reduced to $900 by January 1939. The Fort Worth Boys' Club Council officially incorporated that month as well, their application having been approved by the state on January 24. Attorney J. A. "Tiny" Gooch suggested that the ladies incorporate their council as a non-profit corporation so they could solicit gifts, which would be tax deductible. "The purpose of this corporation shall be to support a benevolent, charitable, educational undertaking, to assist in carrying on the work of conserving the boys' life of the City of Fort Worth, Texas and providing opportunities for the intellectual and spiritual, the physical and social development mostly of underprivileged boys in such community."[2]

The club's budget request to the Community Chest totaled $9,400, which only covered salaries and maintenance. Expenses for the building, equipment, special activities, etc., had to be supplied by the ladies' council and the men Kiwanis.[3]

J. A. "Tiny" Gooch who supported the club as legal advisor and as Santa accepts an award. Seated to the right is Dr. Abe Greines, president of the Fort Worth Boys Club for thirty-eight years and co-partner as Kiwanis Club representative with Hazel and her ladies from the Council. Courtesy Fort Worth Public Library.

Hazel, with her mother, attended her first Boys' Clubs of America, Inc., convention in New York City May 15–18, 1939. It was the thirty-third annual convention for the organization, but it would be the first of nearly fifty such conventions that Hazel would attend in the coming years. Hazel and Bess rode a bus to New York. Miss Martha Justice, who continued to work at the Panther Boys' Club, was active in Boys' Clubs of America, Inc.

One of the speakers at the convention was R. K. Atkinson, former educational director of the organization. Hazel and Bess bought two copies of Atkinson's new book, *The Boys' Club*, which he autographed for them. When Hazel returned to Fort Worth, she read the book carefully, marking passages throughout. A sheet of paper that she placed in the book became yellowed with age. On it she had typed: "Mr. R. K. Atkinson, a Pioneer in the Boys' Club work states: 'In a number of instances, women of exceptional attainments hold important positions in leadership of this type of boy. And in some clubs, they have made a significant contribution as executives. The boy does appreciate the understanding and mother-touch.'" Then she paraphrased a paragraph on page forty-seven of the book: "So, I, like the other women serving as executives in the field, have a faith in my job and realize that the typical Boys' Club member does not have a father who is a leader in the philanthropic, social and business life of the community and our boy has not been able to press his own claim. Youth of today will make America fifty years from today and we have a great responsibility."[4]

One of the chapters in Atkinson's book suggested that the boys "learn by doing" in democratic activities. Hazel was right on track. In January of that year she had proposed that the boys elect a Fort Worth Boys' Club mayor. Actually, the idea for the mayor had come after the boys attended a showing of the movie "Boys' Town" late in 1938 as guests of the Parkway Theater. The first mayor was sixteen-year-old Otis Snow, one of the original 205 members who came that first day in 1935. Otis won the election by seven votes, in a race that included Malcolm Williams, Olin Eddelman, and Bobby Martindale.[5]

Each year when the Community Chest held its fund-raising drive, officials asked the various agencies to write a story explaining what their agency did. With Mrs. Leigh's help, Otis Snow, as mayor, explained the club activities in a newspaper article. In his article he included the Fort Worth Boys' Club pledge:

As a member of the Fort Worth Boys' Club,
I will stand for the manly thing at all times:
I will be helpful in every way;
I will be kind, live pure, speak true, right wrong and play the game squarely.[6]

As part of the war effort, there was a national recognition that the United States must produce more airplanes and a general awareness of aircraft. Boys like to make model airplanes. With all the talk of needing more airplanes to sell to Europe and for U.S. defense, the boys' interest intensified. Besides that, a local airplane factory, Bennett Aircraft, soon to become Globe Aircraft, had been established on the former John Kennedy farm on Blue Mound Road on the North Side, as well as the huge "Bomber Plant" west of Fort Worth. Thus, model airplane contests at the club created new excitement. Soon they had a junior aviators club, and participants could "earn their wings."[7]

William H. Fuller, manager of Municipal Airport (later Meacham Field) agreed to come to the boys' club on a Saturday morning to speak and to judge the model airplane contest. Fuller had been a pilot in World War I and was instrumental in working with the city to create the Municipal Airport in the

During World War II the boys learned to make model airplanes. Mr. W. H. Fuller from Meacham Field came by to instruct. Courtesy Fort Worth Public Library.

1920s. During the summer Fuller even returned on Friday afternoons to teach classes in model airplane building.[8]

Again in May Hazel attended the annual Boys' Clubs of America, Inc., convention, held this time in Boston. After leaving the convention Hazel visited thirteen other boys' clubs; two new ones had buildings costing from $350,000 to $500,000. On her way home she visited Niagara Falls, Hull House in Chicago, and some boys' clubs in Canada. R. K. Atkinson, whose book she had purchased the previous year, had suggested that she visit clubs as "part of my in-service training." She visited the Boys' Clubs of America, Inc., office and asked about the Fort Worth Boys' Club application for membership in the national organization. She was told that their application might not be considered for several months.[9]

The FWBC board knew that their application for membership in BCA, Inc., initiated two years earlier, had been rejected. Alexander Campbell suggested a larger board of directors. The FWBC board voted to continue with their six directors and advisory board because it had "proven very effective." Dr. Greines, in June 1941, wrote the BCA, asking why the FWBC application for membership had not been approved. He knew the BCA wanted a larger board but told them, "We have a governing board of six people, an advisory board of 33 people, and behind this we have two organizations of about 100 each. We cannot conceive of any plan which would better our position . . . so have not seen fit to enlarge our board of directors."[10]

David W. Armstrong, acting executive director of BCA wrote a long letter to Dr. Greines on June 24, 1941, explaining three reasons why the national organization would not accept the FWBC as a member:

(1) Control was "entirely in the hands of a very small group....It should represent the various interests contributing to the community fund."
(2) If the board is representative of the community, "when the time comes to raise money" the board will be helpful in the drive for funds.
(3) If one enthusiastic promoter and organizer "such as Mrs. Leigh" may be compelled to withdraw, it is difficult for a board of directors to carry on. She was secretary of the board and executive director of the club. "This is a combination which would be very difficult for any other member of your board to fill."

"We have noted in many years of experience that Clubs which attempt to operate with boards which are too small are not successful over a period of time in securing the interest and support of the community which a good Boys' Club is entitled to." BCA denied membership until "you decide to meet the qualifications of the Boys' Clubs of America for membership."[11]

The FWBC board remained satisfied with their board structure and did not change it; consequently, they did not then gain acceptance into the national organization. To what extent Mrs. Leigh influenced the board's decision cannot be known at this late date. Naturally, she resented the Panther Boys' Club membership in the national organization when the FWBC was not allowed to join. The size of the FWBC board, would remain a controversial issue for a long time.

Mrs. Leigh got a raise in August 1940 to $135 per month, with total salaries for the club per month at $425. These included physical director, $115; shop foreman and truck driver, $60; librarian, $50; game room attendant, $40; and shower room attendant, $25. The librarian took care of 1,300 volumes and assisted the boys with their school work.[12]

On a live radio show in August Mrs. Leigh revealed that of 1,400 boys between six and seventeen enrolled at the club only six had been before

Hazel Vaughn Leigh as she looked in the 1940s while attending TCU to major in sociology. Courtesy Fort Worth Public Library.

the juvenile court so far that year. What the club was doing seemed to be working.[13]

Hazel's separation from Grover appeared to be firm by 1940. About that time she took on a schedule that left her no time to spend with him. She enrolled in classes at TCU to work on a bachelor's degree in sociology. Could the fact that Miss Martha Justice at the Panther Boys' Club held a degree in the same subject from Texas Wesleyan College and was currently in New York working on a master's have had anything to do with Hazel's plans? Hazel had taken a speech class in 1937, but in the fall of 1940, she plunged into a schedule that divided her time between the university and the boys' club. In 1942 Hazel wrote TCU Dean Colby D. Hall asking him not to penalize her for not taking Spanish 21 before her senior year because she was "employed 9 hours per day at the Fort Worth Boys' Club." The registrar approved her request. Her schedule varied; sometimes she took 7:00 A.M. classes at TCU and then tried to get to the FWBC by 9:00 A.M. She would stay until 9:00 P.M. This was probably in the summer.[14] "I'd go home so tired and why I got into that I'll never know."[15] Other times she worked at the club building from 1:00 to 8:00 P.M. after her morning classes. Sometimes she took classes both morning and night. She continued with a load of twelve to fifteen hours each semester or six each summer term until she graduated June 26, 1944. She earned a bachelor's degree, with a double major in sociology and education and a minor in psychology.[16] She made a "C" in that second part of Spanish that she put off until her senior year. She took her sociology, psychology, and education courses in order to work better with the boys at the club, she later explained.[17]

When the United States entered World War II, Bob Machos, one of Hazel's first boys, was a senior at Fort Worth's Technical and Vocational High School, near the boys' club. The senior class heard the declaration of war in the gymnasium on December 7, 1941. When Machos graduated in 1942, he went immediately into the service.[18]

Running the boys' club during the war was difficult because the club lost the government program which had supplied thirty National Youth Administration youngsters and two WPA adults. They lost many volunteer ladies to the Red Cross war efforts; the men also were busy with additional wartime pressures. Consequently, on Saturdays Hazel and the few remaining staff used the older boys to supervise the younger boys. The older youngsters also helped make Christmas gifts for the younger ones. The FWBC boys also collected grease, metal and other materials for the war effort. In addition, the youngsters followed the course of the war on wall maps at the club.[19]

During the first year of the war, Hazel took time off to attend the BCA convention, in spite of her TCU classes. She learned to "tell specifics of what we are doing to interpret Boys' Club in a defense program."[20]

About this time a reporter asked her, "Isn't running a Boys' Club more of a man's job?"

"I don't see why women can't do it just as well as men. There are a lot of Boys' Clubs managed by women, and successfully too."[21]

Hazel's rival over at the PBC, Martha Justice, would operate it herself as executive director for at least three years during the war while the men were away. Dr. J. H. McLean, still president of the PBC board, announced in 1942 that because four male staff members had left to join the armed services, Miss Justice would serve in the director's position "for the duration." Miss Justice planned to hire part-time workers to carry on.[22]

The article announcing Miss Justice's promotion said that she had the "distinction of being perhaps the only girl director of a boys' club in the country." One can imagine how this news item *did not* go over well with Hazel, because she had been a paid executive director of the FWBC since 1938. One technicality was that the FWBC had not been accepted for membership in the national BCA organization and the PBC had. Hazel saved newspaper clippings to make comparisons between the FWBC and the PBC and noted those attending a PBC summer camp. She fumed about needing a summer camp for her boys.[23]

"Boys aren't problems; they just have problems," Miss Justice told a reporter. She said that sometimes she had fifty opportunities a day to help a boy solve a problem and to help create good citizens.[24] One article about Miss Justice said that every Friday afternoon she wrote letters to each of the 193 former members of the PBC who were presently in the armed services. Hazel kept her own list of the FWBC boys who were in the service, mailed a newsletter to them, and saved the letters the boys wrote back to her. Corporal Otis Snow wrote, "Dear Mrs. Leigh and Boys," from the Hawaiian Islands in 1943 telling her he "wished he could of been there" for the annual birthday party of the club. For the seventeen- and eighteen-year-old club members, "pre-induction training courses" were scheduled for boys "on the threshold of being inducted into the armed forces."[25]

Because wartime conditions made the River Oaks and Castleberry schools overcrowded, one group got out at 12:30 P.M. each day. The club began running two shifts as well as the schools. The FWBC bus picked boys up at that time and returned them to school at 3:00 P.M., about the time that their parents got off work at the bomber plant (by 1942 called the Consolidated-Vultee Aircraft Corporation). Then the FWBC bus picked boys up in North Fort Worth and brought them to the club.[26]

During the war Mrs. Leigh spoke on local radio stations, answering questions about what she was doing "in this national emergency in training youth for American citizenship." Sometimes Mrs. C. A. Lilly, president of the Girls' Service League, would be a guest on the same programs.[27]

Increased activity and unforeseen events on the North Side made life more difficult for the people living and working there, for her boys, and ultimately for Hazel. More than 5,000 workers traveled to the "yards" each day in 1941 and this number increased as larger numbers of animals arrived. Complicating things was a flood, which swept through the stockyards on April 19, 1942, covering the floor of the coliseum and the first floor of every building near North Main and Exchange. A dam at a cement plant upriver had broken. Homes of some of the boys flooded as well.[28]

Then came a disagreement in the club's leadership. The board had raised Hazel's salary to $150 per month, and Dr. Greines, with whom Hazel always worked closely, opposed the move. At one point she wrote him a letter of apology, however: "I deeply regret that you were offended by the action taken by our Board of Directors at the meeting yesterday. Since you feel the way you do about it, both Miss Nolan and myself shall decline to accept the salary raise allotted for the month of September." Dr. Greines's objection must have been expressed that as price freezes were in effect all over the country during the war effort, why not at the club?[29]

When Hazel seemed to be the busiest with her college courses and her shifts at the FWBC, tragedy struck. Grover was hit by a train, suffering a possible skull fracture and a broken hip and leg. He died at 1:00 A.M. Thursday, January 14, 1943, in the hospital, about eight hours after being found unconscious. Although they had been separated about four years, with a strain in their relationship much longer than that, he was still her husband. Neither had sought a divorce.

Grover Cleveland Leigh had registered with the selective service in Tarrant County on May 7, 1942, although at age fifty-three he was not likely to be drafted.[30] Grover had kept up several activities after their separation. He was a member of the American Legion and the Shriners "Ancient Order of Camel Herders." As of January 1942, he was a thirty-second degree Mason of an Oklahoma consistory, Moslah Temple in Fort Worth, and the Patmos Lodge in El Dorado, Kansas.[31] Grover had resigned his job as U.S. Marshal J. R. Wright's chief deputy late in 1942 due to "ill health," which most likely involved his alcoholism.

Section workers of the Texas and Pacific Railroad found Grover late Wednesday afternoon within five feet of the railroad track about one mile west of the Lancaster Street yards. His automobile was parked on Granbury Road about fifty yards from where he was found. The car's gasoline tank was empty, but gasoline ration books were found in the car. Some observers noted that if he had been walking somewhere to get gas, he could not have purchased any without the ration books.

There was a paved road near the railroad track, and the highway patrolman called to the scene commented that he "didn't know why he didn't walk on that" instead of walking on the tracks. There was no evidence of foul play and the death was ruled accidental. Speculation at the time was that he might have been depressed and stepped in front of the train intentionally. His billfold, containing "considerable cash," was in a pocket. Investigators noted that because there was a curve in the track where the incident happened, he might not have heard the train coming. [32]

The first news article of the accident did not mention Hazel, but his obituary called her his "estranged wife" and cited her and his brother as his only survivors. One article indicated that he had planned to accept an Amarillo position. Hazel and her family made the funeral arrangements, and the funeral-home directors gave her the book that people signed, a copy of the service, and so on, which she kept. The lady at the rooming house where Grover lived gave Hazel a gold watch that belonged to him. Hazel's brother Howard paid $186 income tax for the G. C. Leigh Estate on June 15, 1943. [33]

A half century later when talking about Grover to her nurses, Hazel indicated some guilt over Grover, saying she should have talked to him when he wanted to talk. He had apparently tried to reconcile at some point, and she wouldn't discuss it. [34]

Hazel was forty-five years old when Grover died, busy at the FWBC and with her studies at TCU. She seemed to be interested only in those activities and had little time for social life, other than the teas and events of her FWBC Council of ladies.

News articles in 1944 both gratified and frustrated Hazel. The existence of the YMCA, the PBC, and the FWBC in their districts of Fort Worth were cited as lowering the number of "boys in trouble in those areas about 50%" from 1930s figures. Certainly, Hazel was happy with that news. A news item possibly frustrated Hazel, noting that for "the 18th consecutive year" Mrs. R. J. Windfohr would sponsor the Christmas party for the PBC. "Miss Martha

Grover Cleveland Leigh in the 1940s.
He was fifty-four years old when he
died in 1943. Courtesy Fort Worth
Public Library.

Justice, club director" was in charge of arrangements. Mrs. Windfohr was the former Mrs. James Goodwin Hall (Anne Burnett).[35]

The FWBC Council gave its usual Christmas parties during the war. The ladies also purchased a house and lot in 1944 when the FWBC board voted not to do it. The ladies asked if their buying it "would cause any dissension," and the men on the FWBC board agreed it would not. With the additional space, they planned to expand the playground.[36]

Boys home on leave from the service always signed in when they came to the club. Johnnie C. Kohut, USMC, was there on July 18, 1944. Hazel kept a list of the boys who had died: Lawrence Brown, killed in Belgium; David Evans, died in a hospital in the South Pacific; Gordon Goodger, died when his B-29 was shot down over Tokyo; Richard Roden, Gold Star, killed in action.

When Private Otis Snow came home on leave, back from the South Pacific and stationed in the Army Air Corps at Craig Field, Alabama, he led the pledge of allegiance at the flag presentation ceremonies one Monday afternoon for the boys.[37]

Hazel was able to keep in touch with some of her boys without having to read of them in the "missing-in-action" reports. She got a letter from Corporal Snooky Pressley, USMC, Santa Ana, California, bemoaning that he couldn't be on hand at the club's birthday party but requested that "someone eat two servings for him." Billy Burklow was seventeen in 1945 and graduated from high school that year. He enlisted in March; after graduation he worked at the club as an assistant coach for the younger boys, and was called to active duty in August. The war ended before he saw any active service, but he continued on active duty until October 1947.[38]

Mrs. Leigh kept up with all her boys. Snooky Pressley was a professional ball player in 1947. Physical education director C. C. "Corky" Makarwich had predicted as much a decade earlier. Snooky, more formally known as Julian Pressley, played professional baseball for a while, but he went to college and later coached at Odessa Junior High. In the summers he operated a baseball school and scouted for a professional baseball team.[39]

The club boys contributed to the war effort by collecting 19,000 pounds of scrap iron in one drive. In another, the boys went door to door to collect waste fat. A. A. Lund of Armour and Company and Sherman Beasley of the Fort Worth Rendering Company pledged to buy all the waste fat collected for six cents per pound.[40]

Hazel lost her mother Bess Vaughn in 1946. The next year she and her father moved from the Forest Park Boulevard house back to the Vaughn property on Oak Grove Road near Everman, back to the roots of both the Vaughn and Chapman families, where both of Hazel's grandparents and a Chapman great-grandparent had lived. On one of her Christmas cards Hazel included a photo of the beautiful new stone ranch-style house which had a red roof and a two-car garage. She had a longer distance to drive to the FWBC on the North Side, but she loved the quiet retreat. Sam built a house for Howard and his wife, Mickey, as well.[41]

By the late 1940s some of the daughters or daughters-in-law of the original members of the ladies' council had become young society matrons themselves and began working with Hazel to continue to raise money for the club. Virginia King, daughter of Mrs. Farrell, remembered that Hazel was certainly still training the boys to wash their hands and face and brush their teeth. She either got toothbrushes and toothpaste donated by drugstores or raised money to furnish them for the boys. "She taught them to say prayers," Mrs. King recalled.[42]

The PBC and its executive director, Martha Justice, were much in the news in 1947. Just as the Kiwanis Club in North Fort Worth had been partners from the beginning with the FWBC, the Rotary Club of Fort Worth helped sponsor the PBC. Fifteen Rotarians served as directors and advisory board members of the PBC. In early 1947 they planned a $36,000 fund-raising campaign to recondition the Trinity Episcopal Church Community Center that they were renting. [43]

Martha Justice planned her offices in the remodeled educational building of the church. Her plans changed, however. Back in 1942 she had met a young man named Graham Ball who worked for a boys' club in Wichita Falls and had come to tour the PBC. Ball joined the service shortly after that, and they lost touch. When Ball came back from the war and returned to his job as director at the boys' club in Wichita Falls, he and Martha met again at a boys' club regional conference in Laredo and "that's when the romance started."[44]

Martha was Texas area secretary for the national BCA organization at the time. She had been executive-director for the PBC for four years, but she received a twenty-year pin from the BCA in 1946 because she had been working for the PBC since it opened in November 1926.[45]

Graham Ball and Martha Justice married on June 7, 1947, in Wichita Falls. Her sister was her only attendant. After a short wedding trip, she planned to return to Fort Worth to oversee the reestablishment of club headquarters and help the Rotary Club in their campaign to raise the necessary funds. When she had told the board president of her plans on Thursday and got married on Saturday, he asked her to agree to return until a suitable successor could be found. It took about a month.[46] When Martha relocated to Wichita Falls, she became her husband's "helper" at the boys' club there until she retired in the 1960s.[47] "She was my right hand man," Graham said about Martha.[48] The PBC board hired Ira S. DeShazo, former assistant director of the Fort Smith Boys' Club, to replace Martha. He assumed his duties July 21, 1947.[49] Hazel naturally knew of the change in directors at the PBC, but most likely did not acknowledge the event with any wedding congratulations. No one ever accused Hazel of being hypocritical.

Meanwhile she remained busy with boys' club work and other social activities. She was named chairman of publicity for the local TCU chapter of the American Association of University Women for the 1947–48 season. She also was named to a committee to plan the 1948 Sam Vaughn family reunion at Everman.[50]

The boys developed an interest in a new hobby resulting from the promotional efforts of Fort Worth businessman Charles Tandy, who had inherited his leather business from his father, Dave. He produced leather kits—for belts, billfolds, and ladies' purses—including the patterns to be tooled on the leather, pyro-lacing instructions, and the metal tools needed to do the job. He marketed these to veterans' hospitals for the soldiers still needing therapy and recuperation. The leather craft craze caught on in the hobby shop at FWBC.[51]

In March 1949, the mayor of Fort Worth proclaimed the fourth week of March National Boys' Club Week, but the Fort Worth Star-Telegram reporter only discussed the PBC in the story and wrote extensively about the new PBC facilities at 1515 Lipscomb. The article did not mention the FWBC. The news release that sparked the story probably came from the national office. How Hazel felt about all the publicity for the PBC and none for the FWBC, one can only guess.[52]

Following the war, Hispanic-Anglo relations changed somewhat on the North Side. Mexican families, especially some of the young men returning from war, bought houses west of North Main Street. Some Anglo neighborhood groups tried to organize and agree not to sell their homes to Mexicans, but they were not successful. With the post-war prosperity, Mexican families could afford to buy the houses and did. Consequently, Mexican children began coming to the FWBC. In the beginning there were some problems, but as the children were attending school together, they learned to play together at the boys' club as well. The ladies' council bought another lot in 1949 to expand the playground.[53]

The decade of the 1940s was not a good one for Hazel. She had lost her husband and her mother. Then, on July 4, 1949, her brother, Howard S. "Shorty" Vaughn, died. Howard was found unconscious in his damaged automobile on Oak Grove Road, the victim of a presumed accident or foul play. He died later in the hospital, and an autopsy revealed a cerebral hemorrhage had occurred. Howard and his wife, Mickey, had no children, so Hazel had no nieces or nephews. Howard had been a sales representative for National Supply Company, the same company he had worked for when Hazel met Grover, probably through Howard's efforts.[54]

Her work with her "boys" sustained her. To the ladies of the FWBC Council, some of them second-generation members, Hazel repeated, "If you can give them [the boys] a good education, and get them started out right, they are O.K."[55]

For many years the personal satisfaction of working with the boys gave Hazel great joy, although recognition from her peers would have been a nice bonus. In the 1950s this would come.

CHAPTER 9

Professional Recognition

Amon G. Carter, Sr., and Perry Bass may have purchased the facilities for the Panther Boys' Club in 1947, but as a Christmas present in 1950 Carter gave the Fort Worth Boys' Club Council $2,500. Indeed, the council kept busy with their money-making activities for the club. One continuing project was for the women to bring covered dishes and donate food for a downtown luncheon and then serve the men of the Lions or Kiwanis Clubs their lunch for a fee of thirty-five cents (later sixty-five). Whatever business the husbands of the ladies followed, the men were pressed to donate to the club—lumber, carpeting, paint, among other things.

Hazel planned some of the luncheons and teas at her ranch-style home on Oak Grove Road where she showed the ladies a butter dish, syrup pitcher, cake stand, silver service, and some old walnut furniture that her great-grandparents brought to the area before the Civil War.[1] When she sold about fifty acres of the land for development, the buyers agreed to name one of the streets Hazel Leigh Lane.[2]

When the Fort Worth Boys' Club celebrated its sixteenth birthday, Bill Burklow was back helping blow out candles, having driven in freezing rain to be with the club on Tuesday, February 13, 1951. The celebration had been postponed already because of previous bad weather. Five hundred boys received free T-shirts based on attendance and participation, as was the usual practice. It became an annual event that Mr. Tidball at the New Isis Theatre would give the boys a free movie for the birthday party each year. For the sixteenth they saw "Cave of the Outlaws."[3]

By the mid-1950s youngsters were joining the club whose fathers had been members when it first opened. Hazel felt like a grandparent! She kept up with her boys through letters and newspaper clippings, planning to spend all her time at retirement pasting up scrapbooks. One young man whose career she proudly followed was Darrow Hooper, who in 1952 participated in the Olympics in Helsinki as a member of the U.S. team, placing second in shot put. Hooper had been a member of the FWBC seventeen years before at age seven.[4]

In March 1952, the club completed the addition of a 25' x 45' room to the west of the boys' club building to be used for athletic banquets and other activities. Most of the labor was donated.[5]

After nearly twenty years of operation of the club, Hazel told someone, "We've been fortunate. We've had no serious casualties, no more than a few broken arms and legs." The boys operated lathes, jig saws, electric sanders, and band saws. They made lamp bases, chairs, tables, birdhouses. The staff would rush anyone who was injured across the street to Dr. Abe Greines's office.[6]

Hazel was not too thrilled when boxing became one of the activities for the club, but "golden gloves" competitions were becoming popular in the city. Mr. Lupton, Mr. Weekley, and Mr. Farrell bought the boxing trophies for the boys. Other contests continued as well, allowing numerous boys to win prizes. Jerry Crowder, age ten, won the annual freckle contest in 1953 over 25 finalists, narrowed from 175 original contestants.[7]

In the summer Hazel bemoaned not having a summer camp for the boys. The PBC enjoyed a facility at Lake Worth and utilized other facilities through the years. The FWBC took the boys on outings to Forest Park during the summer days. The ladies made and brought sandwiches on these and other excursions. Someday, they would have their own camp. Someday.[8]

Hazel lost her father in October 1955. Her second cousin, Juanita Vaughn Garrison, was with Hazel when Samuel Harrison Vaughn, Jr., died October 19, 1955, at age eighty-two. He had retired only the previous year from the Sam Vaughn Company. The FWBC closed during the funeral. Hazel had considerable business to take care of when her father died, but he had told her earlier not to try to run his business.[9] "You have plenty to live on," he had told her and suggested that she let his one employee, Abe Martin, keep running the business for three to six months until he could get permission from the agency to become a dealer and sell the aeromotor windmills himself.[10]

Hazel believed that Public Law 988 of the Eighty-fourth Congress was the most important document in the history of the national boys' club movement. When President Dwight Eisenhower signed it into law on August 6, 1956, a congressional charter was granted to the Boys' Clubs of America, Inc.

Finally the Boys' Clubs of America recognized the Fort Worth Boys' Club as eligible for membership. Presenting a certificate to Mrs. Leigh and Dr. Greines is regional director Horace Craighead. On Craighead's left is W. M. Green, president of the Kiwanis Club of North Fort Worth. Courtesy Fort Worth Public Library.

Massachusetts had chartered the national organization originally, but the new law made the BCA the only all-boys organization chartered by Congress since the Boy Scouts obtained a federal charter in 1916.[11] John Gleason, national director of the BCA when it was officially chartered, made a concerted effort to organize new clubs across the country. As a result, the FWBC was accepted into the national organization for the first time. Hazel had been trying for nearly twenty years to have the FWBC accepted by BCA.

FWBC accepted its charter in 1957 in Bartlesville, Oklahoma. Hazel traveled to Bartlesville to receive the national membership officially, because she had lived there for nearly two years with Grover. Once FWBC was accepted into the national organization, Hazel persuaded the BCA, Inc., to credit her prior service with the FWBC and start it at 1935 instead of 1957; consequently, she would be eligible for a BCA twenty-five-year pin in only three years.[12]

Hazel enjoyed the national acceptance and recognition for the FWBC and especially looked forward to attending the fifty-first annual convention of the BCA at the Hotel Statler in Detroit, Michigan, May 12–16, 1957. She had been attending for eighteen years herself.[13]

Gary Reagan, Robert Sprinkle, and Tony Scarborough with Mrs. Leigh witness as Governor of Texas Price Daniel, left, proclaims Boys' Club Week. Courtesy Fort Worth Public Library.

Because Hazel was eager and willing to serve, she was named to the national program committee on group methods for BCA. Former President Herbert Hoover, chairman of the board of BCA, and other officials, Albert L. Cole, national president, and John Gleason signed her certificate of appointment.

This time when Governor Price Daniel of Texas proclaimed April 1–7, 1957, as National Boys' Club week in Texas there was no slighting the FWBC in favor of the PBC, as had happened in the past. In fact, to help celebrate that week Mrs. Leigh took three youngsters to Austin on Wednesday, March 27, to be in the governor's reception room when Daniel made the proclamation for the special week in Texas.[14] The three boys who met the governor with Mrs. Leigh were Gary Reagan, Robert Sprinkle, and Tony Scarborough.

Back in North Fort Worth, Hazel secured plenty of publicity for the club because of Boys' Club Week. The April 1 *Fort Worth Star-Telegram* featured a flag ceremony in the gym and a "What's in Your Pocket" contest with prizes. On April 2, a pet parade with prizes in each division was featured; on April 3, arts and crafts demonstrations; April 4 and 5, table tennis and checkers contests with prizes. It all culminated on Saturday, April 7, with a trip to Mrs. Leigh's farm for a kite-flying contest.[15]

With her national affiliation secure, Hazel enrolled in a BCA training course in 1958 at New York University. Of fifty-two participants, forty-nine were men. The two other women were a cooking instructor and a graduate student. The BCA had arranged for the men to stay in the YMCA, but Hazel had to find a hotel.[16]

National affiliation meant that BCA "Golden Boy" awards could be presented for service to the FWBC. The club held ceremonies in April 1959 to present a twenty-year service award to J. A. "Tiny" Gooch for his activities as Santa Claus each year at the Christmas Party and for all the free legal advice he had given the club.[17]

Also in 1959, Governor Price Daniel appointed Hazel to the Texas committee to plan for the 1960 White House Conference on Children and Youth. Committee chairman was Dr. Guy Newman, president of Howard Payne College at Brownwood. The conference met every ten years to deal with problems of young people.[18]

Hazel may have solicited help from important people like senators and congressmen for her club. She would not have hesitated to do so if she thought it would help. Perhaps they were only responding to her requests, but Senator

Still playing Santa in 1952 is J. A. "Tiny" Gooch. Courtesy Fort Worth Public Library.

Lyndon Baines Johnson (at the time a candidate for the Democratic nomination for president) wrote her that he wished "to be of any help that I can to your group." Jim Wright, who also was running for reelection, promised to "be of assistance in any way possible." Perhaps their notes were in conjunction with her participation in the national White House Conference on Children and Youth.[19]

Honors and awards continued to come Hazel's way. In May 1960, at the Waldorf-Astoria Hotel in New York City, she received the Golden Boy Award of the Boys' Club Professional Association for twenty-five years of "the highest ideals of dedicated service" to boys. With 3,000 members in the FWBC, it ranked as the fourth largest club in the Southwest. She was recognized as the only woman executive director of a BCA club.[20]

A major effort that began early in the 1960s was to build an Olympic-sized indoor swimming pool for the boys. The boys had used Marine Park, across the street from the club, but were only able to do so in good weather; this arrangement simply was not satisfactory. Once the FWBC board agreed to work toward that goal, Hazel, as president of the FWBC Council, made fundraising a major effort. Wealthy women were persuaded to hold silver teas in their showplace homes. Sometimes 200 women would buy tickets to attend an event just to see the fancy house. Minnie Meacham Carter, Amon G. Carter's third wife (and widow), hosted a brunch at her home.[21]

Persuading famous people to come to the club when they were in town generated interest in the club among local people. Rex Allen was in Fort Worth to sing at the Southwestern Exposition and Fat Stock Show in February 1960, so Hazel or someone invited him to visit the boys at the club. They made him an honorary life member.[22]

Another way to call attention to the club and raise money for the swimming pool was to auction footballs autographed by TCU football players, popular high school athletes, the Dallas Texans, and the new Dallas Cowboys football team. The auction of eighty-five footballs took place at Clark's Discount Department Store on North Main Street, the building that later became Billy Bob's Texas nightclub. In June 1962, the FWBC Council hosted an antique sale and show to raise money for the swimming pool. Some 225 members attended.[23]

Hazel made a long list of names of people who pledged to give money for the swimming pool and then checked them off when they gave. The pledges ranged from $5 to $30,000. The FWBC Council contributed the $30,000; the

Terry Barber, pitcher for the Los Angeles Dodgers in 1961, autographed a photo to Mrs. Leigh and the Fort Worth Boys' Club. Courtesy Fort Worth Public Library.

Kiwanis Club of North Fort Worth gave $20,000. Hazel donated $5,000 herself, and most of the large donors were members of the council and their husbands. Hazel admitted that she "happily risked being called a pest" as she begged money from civic or church groups and free labor from union locals.[24]

Groundbreaking ceremonies for the new pool took place on Sunday afternoon December 10, 1961, as Dr. Abe Greines and J. Lee Johnson III each wielded shovels simultaneously. Dr. Greines also served as master of ceremonies on Friday evening, July 20, 1962, when the dedication of the new indoor pool took place. The reigning Miss Fort Worth, Patricia Bray, sang the "Star-Spangled Banner," and the current FWBC "Boy of the Year" Charles Brown led the pledge of allegiance. Dr. Greines read a telegram from former President Herbert Hoover and called Mrs. Leigh the FWBC's "guiding light through twenty-six years of service." Eight young boys swam the length of the pool demonstrating the various strokes in an inaugural swim.[25]

The new swimming program included beginning, intermediate, advanced, handicapped, life saving, diving, team and free swim categories. From the 3,202 boys who were members in 1963, the club had organized eight football teams, thirty-two basketball teams, eight softball, and ten baseball teams on an intra-mural basis. They did not play games with the Panther Boys' Club, even though it and the FWBC were the only ones in town. Hazel never did want to talk about the PBC. "Let them do what they want; we'll do ours," she would say.[26]

Hazel later would be named to a three-year term on the national program committee of aquatics of the BCA. Her duties were to help plan and develop program material for use in boys' clubs throughout the country and to partici-pate in research and study projects.[27]

Hazel's mother previously had been active in Democratic Party politics, so Hazel made sure that Texas politicians Vice President Lyndon B. Johnson and Congressman Jim Wright continued to be aware of the FWBC. Her name and address were familiar to local Democratic politicians as well. Consequently, she was one of a large number of people invited to a dinner for President John F. Kennedy to be held Friday evening November 22, 1963, in Austin. Of course, the event was canceled when Kennedy was assassinated earlier in the day in Dallas, but Hazel had not planned to attend anyway because she had not returned the $100 contribution card and a request for tickets. She later wrote on the invitation in pencil: "Knew Pres. Johnson when he was in charge of N.Y.A. Program at Austin, Tex. & we had N.Y.A. Program at B.C. Pres. Johnson asked me to invite Texas guest for Coffee at his office when at White House conf. in 1960. He gave us gold charm with his hat on it."[28]

Mrs. Bert Weekley, FWBC Council secretary-treasurer, used audits made by an accounting firm to total the contributions that the council had made to the club from its inception in 1935 to the end of 1964. The ladies' club contri-butions totaled over $123,000.[29]

Hazel returned from one of her boys' club conventions with the informa-tion that the ladies should start an endowment fund for the Fort Worth Boys' Club and incorporate it with the state. She knew that some of the ladies in the council and their husbands wanted to remember the boys' club in their wills, and she had learned that an endowment for the club was the proper way to handle such matters. The ladies asked the advice of their lawyer, J. A. Gooch, and authorized him and two other attorneys from his firm, to act as agents to create the fund as a non-profit organization. Consequently, the Fort Worth Boys' Club Endowment Fund, Inc., was incorporated January 13, 1964.[30]

Fort Worth Boys' Club Basketball League, January 10, 1959, in cooperation with the Kiwanis Club of North Fort Worth: Mr. W. M. Green, principal of Sam Rosen Elementary, is team manager. Left to right—Sammy Carver, Charles Felan, Floyd Stone, Ronald Baadsquad, and Ronnie Williams; bottom: Gary Reagan, Ronnie Sprinkle, James Stout, and Joe Williams. Courtesy Fort Worth Public Library.

Some have claimed that Hazel chose members for the FWBC Endowment Fund board whom she knew felt the way she did about the club. However, in the beginning, the board members included the six FWBC directors and the presidents of the First National Bank, Fort Worth National Bank, North Fort Worth State Bank, and Ridglea Bank. The three ladies from the council on the FWBC board had remained the same for many years—Weekley, Lupton, and Leigh. Dr. Greines still represented the Kiwanis and was president, but West Hickey and M. B. Fleet were the Kiwanis men on both boards.[31]

In 1966 the land on which Hazel's great-grandfather Chapman settled in 1855 was taken into the city limits. Taxes skyrocketed so much that she decided to sell the remainder of her property to a developer, Home Investment Company, and the new addition of thirty-five acres or so became Highland Hills. A portion of Loop 820 eventually crossed what had been her land. When she sold her land and home, she moved into an apartment at 1703 Hulen Street. She carried with her antiques of every description, including a pistol, which had belonged to her great-grandfather, and her great-grandmother's set of silver made in Montreal before 1845. Her stone home on Oak Grove Road became the parsonage for Highview Baptist Church.[32]

While Hazel had lived south of Fort Worth she had passed near the Southwestern Baptist Theological Seminary every day on her way to and from work. As a youngster she had been raised a Baptist. She formed the habit of contacting the seminary for young students who might like to work part time at the boys' club while enrolled there.[33]

Apparently in 1967 Hazel began thinking of retiring as full-time executive director of the FWBC. After all, she was seventy. She wrote officials of the BCA for help in trying to find someone, but was informed that it would be "in fact almost impossible" to find someone "for the amount of money you are willing to pay." Hazel had been working for a much lower salary all those years than that paid most men directors with families to support.[34]

That bit of news was disillusioning. Something else that no doubt upset Hazel was an article she saved from the official journal of the BCA about women's auxiliary organizations. The article listed functions of the auxiliary (which the FWBC Council technically was) as: complement budget with fund raising, host receptions for staff and board meetings, assist in decorating and refurbishing boys' club building, even give direct volunteer service to the boy members." The article continued: "By no means should an Auxiliary ever assume that it has any authority in the conduct of Club affairs—the administration of the Club must be left to the discretion of the professionally trained and experienced staff, and sovereignty in Club matters lies ultimately with the executive board." Its services are "auxiliary" as its name "implies."[35]

Hazel did not like that article at all, but she had justification for her wrath. The ladies' council (with the Kiwanis Club) had started the FWBC and jointly formed the executive board that ran it. Besides that, the "professionally trained and experienced staff"—mainly Hazel—was on the executive board and president of the "auxiliary" ladies' council. It was complicated, but certainly not the same situation as the ladies' auxiliary clubs discussed in the article. For example, the FWBC board would discuss the need for a bus. The ladies on the board would suggest that the council probably could contribute to the project, would present the idea at the next ladies' council meeting, and then report at the following FWBC board meeting that the ladies agreed to pay one-half the cost of the bus.[36]

A Fort Worth Boys' Club bus picked up boys after school from area elementaries and brought them to the club. Courtesy Fort Worth Public Library.

Later problems for Hazel and the ladies would erupt when the members of the FWBC board, the United Way funding organization, BCA officials, and others did not understand that unique relationship between the FWBC Council and the FWBC, a relationship that had begun decades earlier. Some felt that Hazel's unusual situation was "tolerated" in the national boys' club movement because of her sex and age. She generally was the only woman executive at the meetings of directors of boys' clubs throughout the nation. (Martha Justice Ball always attended with her husband, however.) Hazel believed that she made friends and was supported for her efforts.[37]

The delegates from the two Fort Worth boys' clubs (FWBC and PBC) did not go out to eat together or associate at out-of-town conventions as one might expect. By the 1960s Michie Brous had become executive director of the PBC and would continue in the job for more than a quarter century. Brous had his own friends and Hazel had hers at the conventions. Hazel usually invited another woman to travel with her. Barbara Wheeler or Mrs. C. A. Gilliam sometimes joined Hazel on trips. Hazel loved to travel and once went to Puerto Rico after a convention. Another time she visited a World's Fair. She even went to England to trace the Leigh ancestors and found a Lord Leigh. At some point she went to Honolulu, Hawaii.[38]

Whether or not the men who were executive directors in the other boys' clubs respected Hazel as much as they should have, there is no doubt that they all knew who she was. In most cases she had served longer than any of them. She had worked for lower pay and had spent more volunteer hours through the years. Many of the men probably felt called to their job and cared immensely for the boys in the clubs they served, but it would be difficult to find any who cared more deeply than Hazel Vaughn Leigh or who believed more in the importance of the contribution they were making to youth in their communities. No one ever questioned that quality about Hazel; she loved those boys.

In 1966 FWBC worked on a ten-year plan for the club with the possibility of creating other clubs in Sansom Park and Lake Worth. Also starting in March 1966, with the organization of the officers and board for the endowment, there would be three organizations relating to the boys' club on whose boards Mrs. Leigh would serve: FWBC, Inc., as secretary; FWBC Endowment Fund, Inc., as secretary; and FWBC Council, Inc., as president.[39]

Hazel learned in 1969 that the considerable estate of Mrs. Myrtle Bryenton would donate a large sum of money to the club and that Mrs. Bryenton's wish was that a chapel or auditorium of some kind be built in a suitable place. A suitable place might be at the summer camp that Hazel had wanted to acquire for many years. At last, means to create the camp were emerging.[40]

CHAPTER 10

Finally, a Camp at Eagle Mountain

*H*azel's dream of a camp for the boys—a place on the outskirts of Fort Worth for Saturday and summer excursions, overnight trips, week-long camps— would reach fruition toward the end of the 1970s. Hazel would be officially retired and about eighty years old by the time the camp opened. If you live long enough, and work hard enough, dreams can come true.

First came the hard work, the official retirement at age seventy-five, and then the difficult job of turning the club over to hired directors who saw it as a job rather than a life's work. Before these developments occurred, however, work at the club continued. A new teenage room was built in 1970. The Endowment underwrote the project, and the FWBC board authorized Hazel to contact Preston Geren, Jr., about architectural plans for the room.[1]

Preston Geren, Jr., was the son-in-law of Mrs. Charles Lupton, a longtime supporter of the club, married to her daughter Shirley. Her other daughter, Gloria, was married to Harry Tennison, an official at Coca-Cola in Fort Worth, so through Mrs. Lupton's influence, Coca-Cola sent forty boys to camp at Glen Rose.[2]

In 1970 there was an indication of trouble to come because of a difference in generations or perhaps changing times. Mrs. Weekley moved that "staff members be requested not to wear bikinis in swim pool and side burns below the ear and that hair be cut neat [sic] so it will not touch the collar." The rest of the board agreed. The new policy was posted on signs in the building. Schools also fought the problem of boys with long hair before most of them gave up.[3]

Hazel's right eye had been a problem all her life, embarrassing her as a child and annoying her as she grew older. The problem was not really noticeable unless attention was called to it; she wore tinted glasses to hide it. For years optometrists had said there was nothing they could do about the droopy eyelid, but in October 1971 Hazel underwent serious eye surgery, which seemed to help. As soon as she was back at work from the surgery, Hazel was talking both retirement and a boys camp.[4] "I've tried to retire any number of times, but they won't let me," she told an interviewer in 1971. She also commented that what was "most needed for 1971 is a boys' camp."

"We need a lake site large enough for cabins, mess hall, a chapel, athletic fields, and fishing dock."[5] An auditor for the endowment fund requested that the endowment board record a motion in their minutes that "all Endowment Funds be used as Capital Investment," which is what the charter stated; the board complied. Someone pointed out later that the charter did not say that.[6]

The 1972 Annual Report would inform the board that of the more than $81,000 annual budget, over $25,000 went to educational and social activities, nearly $36,000 to physical education, and nearly $25,500 to management—all at a yearly cost of $30 per boy.[7]

At the annual Fort Worth Boys' Club luncheon are Dr. Abe Greines, Mrs. Burford King, and Mr. and Mrs. Waddy Ross. Courtesy Fort Worth Public Library.

Hazel finally retired March 1, 1973, at age seventy-five. She was honored April 10 at the thirty-eighth annual board luncheon where Jim Sperring of Dallas, executive director of the southwest region, BCA, spoke: "I find where your counseling has made good citizens, good fathers, and good family men out of the boys in the Fort Worth Area." Malcolm B. Fleet, vice president of the FWBC board, also spoke and mentioned that during those thirty-eight years more than 300,000 boys had been members of the club she founded, and the investment had reached $400,000. Fleet presented her with a plaque from the members of the current executive board. Dr. Abe Greines, master of ceremonies for the luncheon, had continued to serve as president of the board of directors of the club, although he resigned at the end of that same year himself. He kept practicing medicine, however.[8]

Hazel shed a few tears at the luncheon, especially when she was presented telegrams and letters of congratulation from boys' clubs directors all over the nation. The letters kept arriving for several weeks. Typical was the one that praised her "ability to get others to become interested in the Boys' Club program," and the one from the national director who told her that many lives were "enriched by her efforts."[9]

"It wasn't all success stories," Hazel told a reporter. "We lost some boys, but there were others who have remained our staunch friends for years and served on the advisory board." At her retirement Hazel commented that she would like to enroll in journalism classes at TCU so she could eventually write the FWBC story, and she did indeed enroll.[10]

Shortly after her retirement the FWBC Council presented a portrait of Hazel to hang in the club. Upon presenting it Margaret Owens said, "Club people who view it [the portrait] will say, West Texas style, 'There is a woman who had Grit, Goodness and Gumption.'"[11]

Following her retirement as executive director, Hazel remained on the boards of all three organizations having to do with the Boys' Club: the FWBC board (where she was corresponding secretary), the FWBC Council, and the FWBC Endowment Fund board. She became involved in other civic activities as well. She was appointed to the Fort Worth Public Library advisory board. She maintained memberships in the Law Enforcement Association of Texas, the American Association of Social Workers (a Gold Star member for her years of service in social work), American Association of University Women

(Fort Worth Chapter); Opera Guild, '93 Study Club, Fort Worth Garden Club, TCU Women Exes, Fort Worth Art Association, General Federation of Women's Clubs; and St. Andrews Episcopal Church. Still affiliated with Democratic Party politics, she was invited to Governor Dolph Briscoe's inauguration on January 21, 1975. There is no indication that she attended, however.[12]

Hazel agreed to serve as president of the '93 Club for the 1975–1976 year. The club, an affiliate of the Fort Worth Woman's Club, was organized in 1893. The ladies always adopted a theme or course of study for the year, and during Hazel's presidency it was the United States bicentennial.[13]

In the '93 Club Hazel met Nelda Gregor, who commented that she had worked with a boys' club in Seattle. Hazel immediately recruited her for the FWBC Council, and Nelda worked for twenty years. The council maintained their fund-raising social activities. In March 1975, they celebrated the fortieth anniversary of the FWBC with a green tea. By this time Hazel generally was cited as "honorary president" of the FWBC Council; other women served variously as the official president. Hazel continued to run the council as she always had done, in spite of no longer being president.[14]

The 1976 bicentennial national celebration inspired numerous commemorations. The ladies created a heritage room or hall of fame at the FWBC to honor outstanding alumni. It was also used as a place to keep their files. The ladies kept the FWBC Endowment Fund records in a locked steel cabinet in that room.[15] C. Darrow Hooper and Yale Lary were among the alumni honored in the hall of fame. Hooper was an outstanding athlete at Texas A&M and won a silver medal in shot put at the 1952 Olympics; Lary had an outstanding career in professional football with the Detroit Lions.[16]

Personnel problems and personality clashes arose between the FWBC board, the FWBC Council, and some of the executive directors at the club in the first few years after Mrs. Leigh retired. Without mentioning specific directors by name, the point can be made that they were young, poorly paid, less experienced than Hazel, and they considered the job a stepping stone to a better job. Hazel and her ladies did not think that the young men were doing an adequate job. Impromptu visits by some of the ladies resulted in complaints that things were messy and not picked up. Hazel believed that the boys' club should be open when the boys got out of school because their parents worked until 5:30. When the club closed earlier, she was displeased. Hazel made a list and reported to the board some items missing from the club: two oil paintings, one boys' club seal, one metal magazine rack, one Ranch Oak coffee table, one chair with red upholstery. Another thing that upset some of the ladies was that the directors did not use all the same volunteer instructors, such as in art or music, that Hazel had used.[17] Documentation exists that in some cases the directors were not as efficient as Hazel had been.

Hazel must have complained about the situation either at one of her national conventions or by letter. Jim Sperring, regional director of BCA, told her: "I think that before too long, Hazel, all the little problems (or at least you think they are problems) will be ironed out and the Club will be flourishing again as it was during your hey day."[18]

The several young men who consecutively served as executive directors in the first few years after Hazel retired probably felt intimidated by her continued involvement with the club. A normal situation would be for an executive director to communicate problems and requests to the board of directors and to make requests and recommendations to them. A board generally

Yale Larry, halfback, Detroit Lions, autographed a photo to Mrs. Leigh and the Fort Worth Boys' Club. Courtesy Fort Worth Public Library.

remained aloof and made decisions or set policy. The FWBC board in the Dr. Greines/Hazel Vaughn Leigh days had always been active in the operation of the club. The FWBC Council also took a personal interest in the happenings at the club. For example, in 1976 they spent $3,000 to asphalt the new fenced playground on a lot they bought for $2,000. The next year they spent $7,500 buying an adjacent house and lot.[19]

Employees at the boys' club and alumni knew Mrs. Leigh and some of the board members much better than the constantly changing executive directors. It is not surprising that the young directors somehow felt that the reins of control were not totally secure in their hands and thus complained.

The major funding agency, the United Way, saw the "problems within your organization" as stemming from the specification that half the board members be men and half be women and that "some board members have become involved in the details of the administration of the agency." The United Way committee that investigated the situation in mid-1975 advised that the board members be selected by the "board as a whole" rather than by the ladies' council and the men of Kiwanis and that "you should strive for broad community representation" on the board. "The duties and responsibilities of both the board and the staff should be clearly delineated." A letter suggested that a spirit of cooperation to adhere to the policies should prevail.

United Way certainly had been long-suffering with FWBC. They had made similar requests for years. One earlier letter stated that "Mexican and Negro youngsters attended the club but that no one of these ethnic groups was yet on the board." The FWBC board reminded the United Way that the ladies' council and the men of Kiwanis chose board members from their numbers and "Neither organization have Latin Americans or Negroes on their Boards at the present time."[20]

In October 1973, the FWBC board amended its constitution in an attempt to satisfy United Way. The new bylaws called for a twenty-four-member board, twelve men and twelve women. Kiwanis would appoint six of their own and six from the community. The ladies would appoint eight of their own and four from the community. In order that the board be revolving, one-third were to serve initially for one year, one-third for two years, and one-third for three. No one could serve more than six years and no one could be reelected until one year had lapsed.[21]

In November 1973, the nominations committee offered a new slate of officers. For the first time in at least thirty-seven years, Dr. Greines was not president of the board.[22] "Our committee suggests that the Fort Worth Boys' Club board examine and define the relationship of the Fort Worth Boys' Club Women's Council to the board and to the agency." The special committee of the United Way that was investigating suggested that the FWBC delay submitting their 1976 budget until "the above recommendations have been completed."[23] In other words, do what we say or we may cut your funding, which, of course, the United Way had the right to decide. They controlled the purse. Mrs. Leigh wrote later on the letter, "This is the same as BCA in 1936 which we *rejected.*"[24]

Hispanic and black board members named to the FWBC board by the Kiwanis, as their members from the community, must have known that they were "token," for they did not come to meetings regularly. Mrs. Leigh—even if she was seventy-nine or so—was always present. At one board meeting, only twelve of twenty-four board members were present. In addition, of the newly enlarged board, more women generally attended than men. The Hispanic board member did not attend board meetings for months at a time.[25]

A United Way representative, William Sarsgard, later explained that the United Way made two studies over a three-year period in the 1970s before recommending changes and did not act hastily. He said that the FWBC was in no way singled out. In fact, the PBC faced some of the same problems because the Rotary Club was its sponsoring organization. Other Tarrant County organizations had not changed their boards either. "The boards needed to be bumped up into the second half of the twentieth century to continue to serve the neighborhood successfully," he said. "The neighborhoods of the FWBC and PBC were changing faster than the clubs. They were by the 1970s in strong minority neighborhoods, but tried to keep the balance of boy members at one-third white, one-third black, and one-third Hispanic. In order to keep these ratios the whites had to travel from farther and farther away to attend. Meanwhile, minorities from the adjacent neighborhood were turned away because the club was full," he said.

"We weren't asking all the women to get off, just add a few from the community to represent the area served," he said. He also indicated that the existing FWBC board was too strict in expecting the boys to conform to a dress code. The kids had changed; the world had changed. "All anybody wanted was a little loosening of the restrictions and rules, but it turned into an impasse."[26]

Hazel, Minnie Weekley, and some of the other board members resisted change and sought to keep the Fort Worth Boys' Club the way it used to be.

Hazel knew that trouble was coming over the insistence of another bylaw revision. At one of the ladies' meetings, she and Mrs. Michie explained that the men on the FWBC board asked the ladies to consider taking their name as a club sponsor out of the bylaws (which would cause the council to lose future control). The council voted unanimously not to make any such change in bylaws and, if necessary, to get legal advice.[27]

Doing things Hazel's and the ladies' way—as they had done for forty years—instead of the United Fund's way would eventually have a price, as they would one day learn to their dismay.

The FWBC board did not change enough to please the United Way yet. By 1978 United Way recommended that the FWBC call in the BCA for advice and complained about the "confusion of roles and responsibilities between the executive director and some board members. The loss of four executive directors in same number of years is indicative of the problem." One young executive director was unhappy when two delegates (the director and Mrs. Leigh) were sent to the national BCA conventions, and Mrs. Leigh was the voting delegate. A letter from Tom Daniels, the BCA southwest regional director, ordered the club to restructure its board and added: "By June 2, 1978 you will have outlined the policy whereby Mrs. Leigh can function as a Board Member and not as the Executive Director." Daniels suggested that the board have three members from the ladies' council, three from the Kiwanis, and eighteen business and professional leaders in Fort Worth. Daniels spoke at a dinner to board members of the new Eagle Mountain Club in Azle, Texas, telling them that Mrs. Leigh was retired and should not have any part of the FWBC. The ladies who heard about what he said were incensed and demanded a letter of apology from him. The FWBC board so moved and gave Mrs. Leigh a standing ovation as they thanked her for all her hard work. Hazel never got a letter of apology but did receive a telephone call, which did not satisfy her. The next year at the annual corporate luncheon of the FWBC, Daniels presented Hazel with the BCA Medallion Award for "exceptional dedication and leadership to the Boys' Club Movement locally and nationally."[28]

Were Hazel's shoes too hard to fill? Or was she interfering with and intimidating the young executive directors? Were the ladies complaining too much by comparing the new directors to Hazel? Were Hazel and the ladies really too unwilling to change? All may have been true, although the ladies denied that they were at fault. All of the problems, however, should not be laid on the shoulders of Hazel and her ladies. One executive director left the trampoline out with no one to supervise the boys using it, and the board expressed "a great deal of disapproval." The board recommended that the director be dismissed. One long-time staff member resigned and wrote a letter to the executive director explaining that the executive director was the problem. The director was "rarely here," "constantly on the phone" and "smoking, drinking, and coverups, are not the kind of examples we need." The director "neglected and overlooked" ordering supplies or maintenance for the club. The staff member who resigned said that the executive director's loyalty "does not rest with the club or its Staff." These were strong accusations, but they provide evidence that not all of the club problems resulted from the board's being half ladies' council and half Kiwanis men or from an overly personal interest in club happenings by Hazel, the ladies, or the board.[29]

The United Way committee, however, in 1978 still blamed the problems on outdated policies which required equal representation of men and women on the board, as well as fixed quotas from the Kiwanis Club and Women's Council. The committee recognized that these two groups were instrumental in organizing the club in the 1930s. However, "the agency is now ninety-eight percent supported by the United Way (the community) and, therefore, the rationale for not wanting to restructure the board was not acceptable." The committee was "concerned" that "75% of the boys participating in the agency are non-white while minority representation on the board is limited." Because the FWBC board did not change its structure, "there was no increase in allocation in the 1979 budget," Hazel wrote on the letter. The United Way had been "concerned" for years, but the FWBC board would not change.[30]

Hazel must have wondered if increasing minority membership on the board would cause minority members to work any harder for the youngsters who needed their help than the ladies and Kiwanis had worked for forty years. The FWBC board (mainly the council members on the board) kept stalling but by 1981 agreed to increase the board to twenty-four members, twelve selected by the Kiwanis and twelve by the FWBC Council. This had been done earlier, but the board had reduced the number because of trouble reaching a

quorum. With this many once more on the board, they again had trouble getting a quorum and keeping a full board because of resignations.[31]

United Way was worried that either the Kiwanis or ladies' council could
"exercise control" and so wanted to limit each group to "not more than four
members" of the larger twenty-four-member board.[32]

The BCA and United Way kept complaining that the FWBC board (i.e.,
Mrs. Leigh) did not remain apart from day to day operations of the club. As
Gene Graves, president of the FWBC board explained in June 1978, several
presidents had asked Mrs. Leigh to make the financial reports, as she was "the
only board member familiar with the system . . . . It has been necessary to meet
the United Way deadlines to receive our monthly allocation in time to meet our
payrolls and Mrs. Leigh has been the only one qualified to do so." Graves wrote
that "the last two inexperienced executive directors and secretary have repeatedly called Mrs. Leigh for information and have many times gone to her home
for help on annual reports and program material. She has always helped them."
Graves assured the BCA that Mrs. Leigh would not interfere with a "professional" executive director who knew his job.[33]

One apparently qualified executive director complained that "The Director
is constantly compared to a Director of a by-gone era in results and statistics."
He also regretted the "inability to be one's own man, take the reins and go for
the club under the supervision of the Board rather than one member. I desire
to see increased involvement by the men of the Board."[34]

Apparently by the 1970s many of the Kiwanis members were former
FWBC boys who were in awe of Hazel and deferred to her; thus she always got
her way. The BCA and United Way knew that a broad-based community board
would not be so influenced. Dr. Greines, the strong voice representing the
Kiwanis who had quietly held his own with Hazel and cooperated with her all
those years, was gone. He retired from the board five years before his death but
had remained across the street to give medical aid if needed. Dr. Greines died
November 23, 1978, at the age of eighty-one.[35]

In March 1979, Gene Graves, still president of the FWBC board, wrote
Roger Lohn, a United Way volunteer on the allocation committee, assuring the
charitable organization that "positive steps have been made to solve some of
the problems with many new board members committed to the mission of
the Boys' Club." Graves said that minority board representation had increased,

but fifty-eight percent of the board still came from ladies' council and Kiwanis Club. [36]

In 1979 BCA was using the new concept of area councils as a channel through which ideas, suggestions, and proposals could flow to the national council. The Lone Star Area Council held its first meeting in San Antonio on May 18, 1979, and Hazel attended. In 1979, Hazel also attended meetings of the American Association of University Women, winning their Hercules Award, and was invocation chairman of the local chapter. [37]

BCA official Sperring wrote Hazel: "This is a time for collaboration. Government agencies, United Ways and Foundations look with favor on this type approach. We're missing opportunities if each club proceeds on its own." Hazel underlined the word "missing" in the letter and wrote beside it in ink: "get this."[38]

Rough times continued. Through those turbulent waters, Hazel, the council, and the FWBC Endowment Fund board plunged ahead to buy land and build a camp for the boys. [39] PBC had a camp on Lake Whitney at the time. Hazel and the board members apparently did not know it, but at some point the United Way informed the PBC director: "We don't spend money on camping" and then cut the camping budget out of the club's annual request. Indeed, the United Way had a camping program through which it gave scholarships to low-income youngsters to attend a camp but did not fund a camp per se. [40]

The FWBC Endowment Fund had been from the beginning a fund to assist the club in capital improvements. United Way funds had always been for operating expenses. Hazel remembered a BCA conference during which scarce funding was mentioned and comments made that if United Way funds dried up, government funding would be difficult to get. Hazel's ladies never seemed to have a problem raising money, however.

By the 1970s the endowment included generous donations from the Bert Weekley and Don Hutt estates and Mrs. Myrtle Bryenton's. In fact, only a decade after its creation the endowment fund's statement of assets totaled $382,631.24. [41]

The council set as its goal for the 1970 season the finding of land for a campsite at Eagle Mountain Lake. Endowment board members began looking for land. This early in the decade neither Hazel nor Dr. Greines had retired. Members looked at several places before finding 112 acres near Azle and Eagle

Mountain Lake (on Sandy Beach Road and Boyd Highway), which they purchased at $1,250 per acre. Closing date was October 1, 1975, with the actual price at $140,000.[42] The understanding was that if the endowment purchased the property, it would be tax free. They later were told that they had to pay Tarrant County and Azle ISD taxes. Then in January 1976, an attorney assured them that all three corporations were tax free and could hold property in their name.[43]

The new project was to be called The Fort Worth Boys' Club Outdoor Learning Center at Eagle Mountain. Later the name was changed to Eagle Mountain Boys' Club Center. The ladies were thrilled that the North Side boys who knew only urban life would have a place to learn gardening, animal life, horseback riding, fishing, nature study, and other outdoor sports.[44]

The endowment board underwrote construction of a 70' x 140' lodge, with heavy fieldstone pillars and a wide chimney, comprising 10,000 square feet of floor space. As Mrs. Bryenton had wanted, there was a stage at one end. Mrs. Leigh enlisted Preston Geren, Jr., to draw up the plans.[45]

Hazel had always been good at asking people to donate their services or work cheaply for her boys. Many Fort Worth city officials were former Fort

The multipurpose building at the Eagle Mountain Boys' Club Camp had a large common room with a fireplace and a stage which some of the major donors had suggested. Courtesy Azle News.

Worth Boys' Club boys, so Hazel got them to do road work, fencing, etc., at no cost. One of Hazel's ladies did all the curtains because her husband owned a fabric store.[46] Members of the FWBC Council furnished the kitchen facilities and built a manager's cottage close to the lodge building at a total cost of $44,833. The Boys' Club Alumni Association furnished sports equipment.[47]

Les Peden, a former professional baseball player and graduate of Texas A&M, was named caretaker and unit director. He and his wife were to live in the cottage rent free and take care of the building, act as security officers for the grounds and building, keep the shrubs, and property watered, etc.[48] Hazel's future plans were to build cabins to sleep six to eight boys each. She wanted the endowment or the council to build one cabin a year. "We didn't do it because we got too much flak from the men," one of the ladies complained.[49]

Early on in the project the FWBC Endowment Fund board enlisted the aid of the community of Azle, it being the closest town to the property. Local boys could use the rural outdoor center as well as the urban North Side youngsters.[50]

The endowment technically owned the Eagle Mountain unit and leased it free to the FWBC, representing a $12,500 annual gift in leasing value. The endowment also paid the insurance on the buildings. In 1978, when the facilities were nearing completion, the FWBC board asked United Way to add funds to the budget for the operating expenses for the Eagle Mountain Unit, requesting $32,200 for the purpose. The reply came from the United Way: "We recommend that the Fort Worth Boys' Club Outdoor Learning Center and Eagle Mountain Boys' Club Center not be funded in 1978. . . . The proposed service area is not a high priority area for new social development or social adjustment services."[51]

United Way officials explained that juvenile crime figures were not kept separately by Azle police and were unavailable, although only one child had been referred to the county juvenile probation department in 1976. They said that Azle had not been consulted and involved in planning. A community should show a strong desire for a program before United Way decided to fund. United Way told FWBC to resubmit the request the next year after consulting the community to be served.[52]

One can imagine Hazel's chagrin. The whole point was to construct a camp for the North Side boys of FWBC, not create a club for Azle youth. Having built the club in their area, the endowment was going to be neighborly and let the Azle community use it too. (Perhaps learning that United Way did not fund camps, promoters made the project a "club" for the Azle area.) Even without United Way funding, the endowment carried on and planned the dedication of the facility, which took place on May 16, 1979. J. A. "Tiny" Gooch served as master of ceremonies, and the Azle High School band played.[53]

Azle businessman James Emanuel, whose company constructed the lodge, presented Hazel with a corsage. A local news article reported the ceremonies and that the new facility was free from indebtedness due to the FWBC Endowment Fund. In an interview close to the dedication Hazel told a reporter, "At the going rate of $20,000 to keep a boy in a state institution for a year, I figure we have saved the state hundreds of thousands" (since 1935 when the FWBC opened).[54]

Following the dedication in late May, the doors officially opened on Monday, June 4, 1979. Boys from Azle attended the club that summer. Working parents considered it good day care for the small annual membership fee, which was $2 at first and later $6. Council president Mary Sue Keith engineered several buses and vans to carry boys from the FWBC on the North Side out to the Eagle Mountain Camp.[55]

That fall, the United Way wrote Gene Graves: "Although the United Way has not opposed the Azle expansion, it has repeatedly denied or not considered funding in light of higher community priorities. In retrospect, it is unfortunate that careful consideration was not given to whether operational funds would be available before a major capital effort was undertaken. It is our understanding that the board was prepared to take that risk. . . . A case in point would be the Panther Boys' Club expansion in Burleson which was undertaken only after United Way had committed operational funds."[56]

Hazel and the three boards had gambled and lost. Perhaps it seemed to Hazel that even though the ladies of the council had the money, they had to ask the men first. United Way officials certainly were not all men, but the ladies often referred to them as a group. Through the years the council had not asked anyone's permission. They did what they felt needed doing—buying land and expanding the FWBC, building a swimming pool, etc. FWBC continued to ask United Way for funding for the Eagle Mountain Unit each year—$40,000 in 1980 for the next year. But funding never was approved.[57]

Once everyone realized that no operational funds were available from the United Way, adjustments had to be made. FWBC could divert some of its budget but not much. A large portion of the operating funds would have to be raised locally; the initial need was $21,058. Azle area clubs pitched in— Sertoma, Optimists, and others. Azle residents were named to the board and worked hard. The Azle community held chili suppers and auctions at the club to raise funds Some ladies formed a new Hazel Vaughn Leigh Auxiliary for the Eagle Mountain Boys' Club.[58]

Mrs. Leigh came out to all fund-raising events and brought friends who bid at the auctions, as did she. With limited funds, the local board in cooperation with the FWBC hired a director and planned a recreational program for local boys. By the summer of 1980 there were 500 local boys attending.[59]

Local supporters recall that the FWBC boys did not come out very often in the 1980s. The Azle community had been handed a paid-for facility—all they had to do was provide operating funds to reap the benefits for their youth. They worked hard, but it became more difficult to raise the annual operating budget. Two Azle city officials, City Manager Harry Dulin and City Councilwoman Iona Reed, made a presentation to what by then was the Boys' and Girls' Clubs of Greater Fort Worth to split the difference with them for a $44,000 annual budget. A young Azle bank officer, Tim Carpenter, literally went around town and begged money from banks, businesses, and individuals. Azle raised its $22,000.[60]

During the last two years the facility was open, the Azle community itself put in $40,000. Some money did come from the Boys' and Girls' Clubs. When the Azle community realized that they could not continue raising $20,000 every year, they finally closed the doors in agreement with the Boys' and Girls' Clubs.[61] "There were needy kids who had no other place to go. There really was a need there," Carpenter said.[62]

The club operated for over a decade, but sat empty for a couple of years. In 1995 the Azle Independent School District purchased the Eagle Mountain facilities of a house, club building, several ball fields and 107 acres of land for its state-mandated alternative education program. They later built a new junior high school on the land and a maintenance shop facility, which opened in 1999.[63]

The Eagle Mountain project constructed by the FWBC Endowment Fund is still being used by youth, but certainly not as Hazel, the endowment, and the council had intended. It was supposed to be a camp for the North Side FWBC boys, but it "never really operated as such." Not too long after the Eagle Mountain facility was fully operating, the board structure of FWBC changed: Hazel and her ladies lost their equal voice on the board. The new board members and the staff of FWBC chose not to use the camp. Perhaps Hazel's dream had been too long in attainment after all.[64]

CHAPTER 11

Clashes and Confrontations

"It's got to be half men and half women," Hazel kept reminding members of the Fort Worth Boys' Club at board meetings when anyone brought up the United Way request to broaden the base. Mrs. Leigh sometimes suggested that if the United Way wanted more board members, representation from the Kiwanis Club, FWBC Council, and the FWBC Endowment Fund should be increased.[1] "We need more minority members and members from the community at large," one of the men generally replied.[2] Although the FWBC Council still attracted sometimes 200 ladies to teas, members of the Kiwanis Club of North Fort Worth was getting older, and membership was dwindling. Kiwanis seemed willing to relinquish control to a broader community group, but Hazel and her ladies were not.

Procedures for requesting, securing, and spending improvement funds for the club involved cooperative efforts. For example, when the FWBC board decided to make a capital expenditure at the club, such as repair a roof or fix the air conditioning, the board's ladies who were also on the council or the endowment would go to that group, relate the problem, and a vote would be taken to supply the money. Hazel and some of the other women served on all three boards. Hazel was tight with money, and it generally went for what she wanted. Nevertheless, she wanted to do what was right for the boys and could be convinced to do so. Some thought that she might have complied with United Way requests if more diplomacy had been used. But, unfortunately, there were meetings in which Hazel was not included; some of the FWBC board members were rude and unkind, and she was not always treated fairly.[3] She was once told to "shut up."

When some men who had not been boys' club members and who did not mind disagreeing with her joined the board, things did not go as smoothly. These men pushed harder to comply with the United Way guidelines. Soon, at board meetings ladies sat on one side of the room and men on the other. Hazel tape-recorded the meetings. Hazel also had run out of influence with the United Way. Years before, husbands of some of her council members exerted influence on United Way. In addition, United Way was no longer solely a fund-raising organization but an umbrella agency over other charitable groups. It began to dictate policy. Hazel and her ladies were not alone in resenting the interference.[4]

Hazel noted that some of the members of the larger FWBC board (created to please BCA and United Way) had been absent seven, eight, or nine times. In her mind, this showed that they did not care. Once when they appointed two new members to fill vacancies, Hazel wrote on her copy of the minutes: "Both soon resigned."[5]

In June 1983, more than a dozen ladies of the council signed a letter to their long-time voluntary attorney (and Santa) "Tiny" Gooch. They asked how to change the bylaws to provide that half the FWBC board should be from the FWBC Council and half from Tarrant County at large. They wanted to eliminate the equal participation by Kiwanis because their membership was small and their contributions from 1963 to 1980 small as well. "Although we hold nothing against the club," two or three members "have caused some problems that might become serious." The ladies wrote, ". . . we will not agree to give the Club to the Kiwanians, or to anyone else." They wanted to reach an agreement with the Kiwanians for the bylaw change. The ladies asked if they should buy the Kiwanis interest in the club and then perhaps sell it. The ladies were also concerned about gangs in the area, the FWBC bus not picking up boys in certain areas, and girls coming to the club everyday. "We need your counsel and your help," they wrote Gooch. Eventually the lawyer advised them to get a real estate agent and sell the property the council owned. In light of later events, perhaps they should have immediately taken his advice.[6]

At a September 1983 FWBC nominating committee meeting, the four men and one woman rewrote the bylaws to leave out the Kiwanis and the ladies' council in selecting board nominees, making recommendations entirely the responsibility of the nominating committee.[7]

By October 19, 1983, the president of the FWBC informed the ladies' council that on November 22 the FWBC board would vote on a proposed change in bylaws that would make the board of directors solely responsible for filling vacancies on the board. Hazel asked her friend Bill Hinckley of the Omaha Boys' Club for advice, but he could not make it to Fort Worth. He suggested the leaders of the three "alienated groups" meet to work out their problems, declare a truce, hire someone to conduct a study and perhaps create a "new board organizational structure."[8]

The ladies were further upset October 1983 when United Way asked the FWBC Council for a financial report. The council president wrote a letter explaining that the council was a separate corporation "not supported in any way by the United Way. Therefore, we do not owe the United Way a financial report."[9]

"Mrs. Leigh, it's time for you to quit. Let us name a building after you, and you can sit back and enjoy," one of the men suggested about this time.

"I don't want a building named after me if you men are running it," she replied.[10]

That quick exchange addressed the heart of the problem. If the ladies raised the money, they wanted a voice in how it was spent. The ladies would not vote to change the bylaws to broaden the FWBC board because they would then no longer hold half of the seats, as they had done for nearly half a century.

It took the men two or three years to get enough votes on the board (by persuading some of the at-large members) to change the bylaws.

"It had to be done to comply with United Way guidelines," one of the men explained.[11]

"We had to do it, but it wasn't fun," another agreed.[12]

Hazel also voiced her displeasure at the board meetings over the fact that the club now provided facilities for girls at the club.[13]

According to some people, before the vote to oust the ladies, Mrs. Leigh had thoroughly dominated the board. According to others, she had not. Some said that she explained what she would like to do, and people generally went along with her. Some of the members could convince her of things that needed to be done. Other former boys' club members would resign rather than disagree with her.[14]

The ones who finally engineered the vote to change the bylaws did not have the patience to explain things to Mrs. Leigh and were unwilling to take the time and diplomacy needed to persuade her. They simply plunged ahead, explained some observers. These men were frustrated that the two major capital funding sources for the club (other than the operating budget from United Way) were controlled by Mrs. Leigh and her self-appointed boards. Sometimes wealthy people would write big checks for the boys' club. If Mrs. Leigh got to them before the treasurer of the FWBC board, she deposited the money in the endowment fund rather than the FWBC account. United Way kept asking about the endowment money. "What are you doing with that money?"[15]

"There needed to be more stability. It couldn't operate that way anymore," explained Paul Koeppe, treasurer and later president of FWBC.[16]

So the vote to change the bylaws finally came. It was at the FWBC board meeting November 22, 1983, and the ladies knew they were outnumbered when they arrived. Board meetings had not had a quorum much of the time, but for this vote a roomful assembled.

"I think all of North Side is here," someone said.[17]

One of the ladies informed the assembled group that the council opposed the change in the bylaws and would withdraw their financial support if it passed. Three ladies, including Hazel, did not even vote; they left. The remaining board members voted seventeen to one for the changes, nominated ten new directors, four to take office immediately and six in January.[18]

The council no longer had an equal voice on the board. The ladies charged that many men served on the board for reasons other than to help the boys. Possibly they wanted a community service organization on their resume, or they wanted to meet other men for business reasons, or they wanted to make contacts that would be beneficial later, perhaps in running for office.[19]

At that infamous meeting the FWBC executive director, David Jackson, commended the board for "the action and decisions you have made here today." Jackson had resigned a month earlier, contending that the FWBC board, not the executive director or the consultant to the board (meaning Mrs. Leigh), should formulate policy. "The effectiveness of the FWBC Executive Director must not be interfered with in the management of the day to day affairs of the FWBC by anyone."[20]

Jackson also reported that the council had allocated $10,000 for the construction of a baseball diamond at the Eagle Mountain camp and that the endowment board had appropriated $18,000 to construct a fence to enclose the entire recreation area. The executive director pointed out that "those support organizations had not requested approval or otherwise of those projects by this Board."[21]

Most reasonable people detached from the disagreement could see that both sides had valid concerns. The ladies raised their money, and they wanted a role in deciding how to spend it. However, the FWBC board reasoned that the money was donated for the boys' club, and the board should decide how to spend it. Other priorities might be higher than baseball diamonds and fences at the Eagle Mountain unit.

Money, decision making, and some personality clashes would create much havoc and heartache in the coming years, especially for Hazel. Some participants said that perhaps the FWBC board members should not have plunged ahead, even though the United Way was pushing them to enlarge the board and holding out the carrot of annual funding (or a lack of it) as the incentive.

Immediately after the women lost their equal position on the FWBC board, some of them talked to attorney Emory Cantey, who, like Tiny Gooch, had given the club free legal advice through the years. They asked, "What can we do?" He told them they could sue for control of the club because they founded it, but Hazel did not want to sully the name of the club by going to court. Technically, the "men" did not take over because there were still women on the FWBC board but not an equal number and not all of the women were from the council.[22]

Nelda Gregor, president of the FWBC Council wrote a letter to the FWBC president, Raymond Wilson, informing him that "after serious reflection on our part, we have decided to withdraw our support of the Fort Worth Boys' Club, Inc."[23] In fact, the ladies' council wanted to tear down the old building and build a new one, and they had the money to do it.[24]

A BCA official believed that a broader based fundraising was needed. Hazel could withdraw her support at will. Further, her support, or lack thereof, meant the council's support as well. His implication was that the ladies' support was not enough either.[25]

The next year, Paul Koeppe had to beg the endowment and the council for money to cover a shortfall of $25,019, which the United Way had disallowed in the budget. In the old days, the ladies would have been aware of the shortfall and promptly would have voted the money themselves. In 1984, however, the FWBC had a twenty-four-member board representing the community, as per United Way instructions but had isolated itself from the two previously generous funding sources.[26]

The ladies wanted to say, "Serves them right!" Members of the FWBC board were convinced that "This is the weirdest arrangement ever—three boards deciding how to spend money for the FWBC." It *was* unusual, but it was an arrangement that had evolved over nearly fifty years.

The ladies did not totally withhold their support after the bylaws change. In June 1984 they voted to provide food two or three times a week for boys in the camping program at the Eagle Mountain facility. The ladies objected to giving money directly to the boys' club, though, although the endowment voted $24,500 to repair the swimming pool at the FWBC.[27]

At the FWBC executive committee meeting in July 1984, the point was made that if the three organizations were raising money for the boys' club, they might all ask the same trust or donor and jeopardize future donations.[28]

In December 1984, the ladies discussed dissolving the endowment, distributing the funds to the ladies' council, and starting another boys' club elsewhere. When the FWBC found out that the ladies were planning to dissolve the endowment, they called a special meeting on December 23, 1984. Hazel was asked to the meeting to explain the ladies' plans. She told the group, "The Ellis Avenue Club is not meeting the purpose it was organized for, *to serve boys.* The attendance is low." During 1984, the FWBC changed its charter to say its purpose was to serve "youth" instead of "boys," meaning that girls could be served as well. Hazel reminded them that the endowment charter read to serve "boys."[29]

At the meeting a vote was taken to authorize a lawsuit against the council and the endowment. "The lawsuit was the beginning of the end," one of the ladies explained.[30]

The FWBC obtained a temporary restraining order on January 3, 1985, and an order setting a hearing to prevent the endowment fund from transferring its assets to anyone but the FWBC, Inc.—meaning not to transfer anything to the council. The hearing was set for January 11, 1985, in the 153rd District Court in Tarrant County.[31]

The lawyer for the FWBC wrote the president of the endowment board "the best interests of the boys cannot be served by having the Endowment structured as it now exists." The practice of sitting as a sort of "super council" and "determining how the Boys' Club should be operated and how funds should be spent is quite unworkable." He called it a "technical violation of the trust" to dissolve and turn funds over to the council. He wanted the Fort Worth Boys' Club, Inc., to be able to name directors to the board of the endowment.[32]

FWBC was trying to get a commitment of $20,000 in unspecified operating funds from the endowment. United Way was "very interested in progress reports on the relationships between the Board, the Endowment and the Council." The endowment board's position was that the endowment was organized strictly for capital investment and improvements, new units to the club, and that the income was not for operating expenses of the club. In fact, one of the ladies explained later, "We fought because we wanted the endowment money for the Boys' Club. We figured the United Way would make them use it all for operating expenses."[33]

Much of this controversy resulted because Hazel did not agree that the club was being run as well as it should be. She held that the purpose of the club would not be met if girls became a part of it. On one occasion a frustrated Hazel spoke out: "Listen, let me tell you. If you want a bunch of pregnant girls walking around here, then let them in. You can't keep them apart. They'll be behind the bookcases, or wherever!" The men on the board sat shocked at her outburst. Her ladies agreed with her that the club was not for girls.[34]

Some members of the board suggested that they not buck Hazel and just wait her out. After all, in July 1985 she was eighty-eight years old. However, she gave no indication of backing off or dying soon, and in fact would live to be ninety-seven.

FWBC had operated as a club for boys for fifty years. Ironically, several directors of boys' clubs in the area, all men, later admitted that they did not think girls should be admitted either. In fact, Michie Brous, executive director of PBC for twenty-seven years, retired rather than continue as director when the national organization became "Boys' and Girls' Clubs of America." Brous said that the boys needed the masculine influence they benefited from at a boys' club.[35]

However, the Civil Rights Act outlawed discrimination against girls. Boys' clubs needed government grants; to be eligible, they had to serve girls. In the earlier days neither PBC nor FWBC had accepted federal money.[36]

By mid-July 1985, Hazel had endured enough rudeness and disrespect from the FWBC board. She asked if the ladies ever would be reinstated on the board by revised bylaws and was told "No." Her right to serve on the board for life had been passed many years earlier, but she saw she had no voice. The FWBC board was suing her and the endowment and council boards, so her position was untenable. She resigned. The ladies talked of selling the lots on Ellis Avenue to which they held the deeds.[37]

The court case between the FWBC board, the endowment board, and the council was dismissed on April 18, 1986, by Judge Sidney Farrar, Jr., of the 153rd District Court because the parties had reached an agreement two weeks earlier. The endowment offered thirty-five percent of its net income to the FWBC for general operating purposes and fifty percent of net income for capital improvements and repairs. The agreement stipulated that the president and treasurer of FWBC serve on the endowment board and vice versa.[38]

Hazel wrote letters to her friends in the boys' club movement about what was happening to her. William Hinckley of the Boys' Clubs of Omaha wrote her a long letter of encouragement in August 1986, saying she had "had to endure far more misunderstandings, law suits, debates, attempted takeovers, community battles, board fights and arguments than should have been your lot in life." He assured her that the record would show that she was "always truthful, honest, and straightforward" in all her dealings and that all she and the ladies ever wanted was a first class boys' club . . . . I for one, don't believe you lost the battle . . . your ideas, philosophy, goals, etc. will resurface." Hinckley hated to see Hazel "so angry and bitter over the Boys' Club issue." He urged her not to hold a grudge or let the boys' club events "canker your soul. Walk away from the old problem and start building a new project."[39]

Bill Burklow wrote urging her not to let the events "bother you one iota— you mean too much to us."[40]

An incident in 1986 indicated attitudes on both sides of the controversy concerning Mrs. Leigh's role at the boys' club. The ladies kept their files, the minutes of their meetings, some plaques and memorabilia in the heritage room they had created in 1976. The room became a point of contention between the ladies and the current executive director, William C. Brittain. When the council members came to the boys' club, they found locks changed on cabinets and doors; they were neither given keys nor notified. They complained. Bill Brittain, who had previously worked in boys clubs in St. Croix, Cincinnati, and Louisville, claimed that he needed the room.[41]

"The ladies' Council is giving the club rent free the property we own to the FWBC. If we can't use this room as an office, we will have to rent one," Mrs. Leigh said.[42]

Gene Graves, president of the FWBC board at the time, instructed Brittain to leave the room under Mrs. Leigh's care and let the combination to the lock be known only to her. Apparently this was agreed upon. In the fall of 1985 Mrs. Leigh and Miss Elizabeth Haddaway worked in the room one day and accidentally left Mrs. Leigh's Mexican walking cane there. Later Brittain telephoned Mrs. Leigh to say that he needed to get in the room. She gave him the combination when he gave her his word that "nobody but him would have the combination or enter the room." Following an awards luncheon on November 22, 1986, Mrs. Leigh asked Brittain if he would get her walking cane from the heritage room.

"Oh, that's now the computer room," he replied.

Mrs. Leigh asked where their files and other things were located and why they had not been notified.

"The board voted it," he replied.

When Mrs. Leigh asked where their materials were stored, he took them to the swimming pool hallway.

"Did the board know the history of the heritage room?" she asked him. "No."[43]

The explanation of the FWBC board was: "We got a grant to put computers in, and they needed to be locked up. That room didn't have a window and could be locked up, so it became the computer room."[44]

The presence of two FWBC board members on the endowment board did not help anything. FWBC treasurer Richard Spraberry moved that the endowment be dissolved and its assets and records given to the FWBC. He and FWBC President Paul Koeppe voted "yes"; ten other endowment members voted "no." Nothing was served by the exchange except more strained feelings. When the frustrated endowment board (at the same meeting) wanted to impose rent on the FWBC for the Eagle Mountain unit, Mrs. Leigh reminded the board that the children were the most important. "The board should not impose a hardship on the boys' club if it could be avoided." The two representatives from the FWBC only came to the endowment meetings for a short while, because there was no point.[45]

When the endowment board objected to something at the club, the attorney for the FWBC reminded the endowment that "the Endowment does not run the Boys' Club." At the same time he threatened more court action if the endowment did not "honor its responsibilities" by turning over thirty-five percent of its income to the club for its operating budget.[46]

Each side began accusing the other of not honoring the April 2, 1986, agreement. The endowment was supposed to turn over thirty-five percent of its interest income to the FWBC but in 1988 only turned over $4,238 and waited until December of that year to give it.[47] FWBC said that the council was threatening to evict the club from the swimming pool because they owned the deed to the land on which it was located. The ladies refused "to provide any of the benefit of the funds raised in the name of the Fort Worth Boys' Club, Inc. to the said Boys' Club," the FWBC board accused.[48]

In March 1988, when the endowment board was threatening to charge rent for the Eagle Mountain property, the FWBC lawyer wrote the endowment directors that "a Trustee with a single beneficiary (Boys' Club) cannot require that beneficiary to pay for the use of property that was donated for its benefit." Hazel explained that gifts to the endowment were mostly from "those who did not want to give to Ellis Avenue Club," and the council organized the endowment because most of the gifts were bequests left by their members. For example, shares of Tandy stock were donated to the endowment "to provide a long-term benefit to your organization as your Board of Directors or Trustees may direct and not for your general day-to-day operations and expenses." The endowment board complained that the FWBC board had failed to maintain the Eagle Mountain property. An attorney advised them that the endowment fund could use money to do the repairs itself.[49]

Meanwhile, at the national level in the boys' club movement, things were changing very rapidly. About sixty percent of the clubs in the western states were calling themselves boys' and girls' clubs. At a national conference of Boys' Clubs of America in Houston, representatives of local clubs brought forward the recommendation that the national organization change its name to Boys' and Girls' Clubs of America, Inc., to reflect what was already happening at local levels. BCA representatives voted to do this. Shortly thereafter the Girls' Clubs of America filed suit in a New York federal court on February 29, 1988, to prevent Boys' Clubs of America from changing its name to Boys' and Girls' Clubs of America, Inc. The Girls' Clubs of America argued that the girls' clubs served a different purpose than boys' clubs and did not want to be merged. Hazel, of course, did not think they should merge either. The case never reached trial but was settled out of court for a large sum of money. The BCA bought the right to use the Girls' name. The separate girls organization took on a new name, Girls, Inc.[50]

Jim Caufield, senior vice president of administrative services of Boys' and Girls' Clubs of America, explained that "times were changing, and it is better to change before being forced to do so by the courts." The issue of boys' and girls' clubs arose in California in the 1970s and was driven by funding sources. Court cases in California and Michigan forced the issue. Most of the opposition to adding girls came from the South and Southwest; most older executive directors were opposed as well. Younger people in the boys' and girls' club movement recognized the addition of girls as "more reflective of contemporary society."[51]

Several members of the boards of PBC and FWBC met at the popular Paris Coffee Shop in downtown Fort Worth in October 1988 and proposed that the two clubs merge effective January 1, 1990. The new name would be Boys' and Girls' Clubs of Greater Fort Worth, Inc. Girls had been attending the clubs for a number of years anyway. [52]

PBC "expressed its resolve" not to finalize the merger until the matters between FWBC and the endowment fund were settled. Meanwhile, the FWBC Council sponsored a style show attended by 304 society ladies and raised $2,000, but none of the money went to the FWBC. Instead, the ladies gave three TWC boys $500 scholarships each.[53]

In February 1989, the FWBC board obtained another restraining order against the endowment and the council charging that:
— The endowment board threatened to evict the FWBC, Inc., from the Eagle Mountain unit,
— The endowment had not managed its funds well,
— The endowment paid accountants rather than take free work,
— The council threatened to evict boys from the swimming pool,
— The council refused to provide any of the money raised in name of boys' club to the club, and
— The council has withheld donations from the Boys' Club.[54]

The order continued that "unless a constructive trust is imposed upon the assets of the Ladies Council, the Ladies Council will be unjustly enriched at the Boys' Club expense." The restraining order stated that "immediate and irreparable harm will accrue to the Fort Worth Boys' Club, Inc., if the Endowment and its Directors, and the Ladies' Council are not restrained, forthwith, without notice or hearing, from disbursing any funds or property to any agency except the Boys' Club." FWBC directors also feared that the "planned merger of the Boys' Club and the Panther Boys' Club may be threatened." The directors of FWBC insisted that they were acting in order to do the best thing for the boys.[55]

One of the attorneys assigned to work with Hazel and the ladies' council on the case in February 1989 was a young lady named Michelle Marti, a distant Vaughn relative. Michelle worked at the law firm Gooch, Cantey and Hanger that had traditionally done pro bono legal work for the Boys' Club and Hazel. Michelle's boss informed her they were not working for free anymore.[56] "Old guard lawyers felt they should do free work for charitable organizations. That's why Tiny Gooch and Emory Cantey did so," explained one of Hazel's ladies.[57]

It took two years to settle the case. At the crux of the matter was the merger with PBC. The council held title to the lots on which the boys' club facilities sat; they had purchased the land outright forty to fifty years earlier. FWBC needed clear title to the property in order to merge. At a hearing, Paul Koeppe admitted that the ownership issue "has to be straightened up."[58]

The council's lawyer argued that FWBC had made no effort, in 1983 or thereafter when the ladies withdrew their support, to get that support back. It was only when they wanted to merge with PBC that they wanted clear title to the property; then they sued the women for it.[59]

Judge Michael D. Schattman on February 28, 1989, dissolved the temporary restraining order and ordered the two parties to begin discussions. Hazel's attorney informed her and the other ladies that the judge's order for mediation was to include the merger of the two boys' clubs as a discussion topic.[60]

In a statement of position, FWBC lawyer Michael Handy, argued that the endowment and council could hardly consider themselves landlords and threaten to charge rent when the properties it held "are in fact trust property which quite simply cannot be jerked away from the intended beneficiaries and given to somebody else." He admitted that feelings were involved, but that "such matters are merely historical and should be put aside" to concentrate on "effecting the merger" so that "better services and more services can be available to the youth of Fort Worth."[61]

Mrs. Leigh was ninety-two, but she took part in negotiations with the mediator in December 1989. She no doubt remembered events of fifty-five years earlier in December 1934, when she and the ladies of the PBC Women's Council were upset because their donations to the club had been sold for salvage and the board had ignored their complaints. She kept clippings of the *Fort Worth Star-Telegram* article of Wednesday, June 21, 1989, which noted that the FWBC board "unanimously" approved a draft plan to merge with "former rival Panther Boys' Club." She understood the rivalry far better than anyone else, for in a large measure, she had caused it. "Everybody really thinks this is the best thing that can happen for both clubs," said Lyn Downing, newly elected as first woman president of the FWBC board.[62]

Jim Stratton, at the time regional director of the new BGCA saw the merger as wise. "The competition with each other [PBC and FWBC] was hurting both clubs in recruiting boys, fund raising, etc. There was confusion of wealthy donors with two clubs raising money. 'I just gave to the boys' club,' they would say." Concerning Hazel, "I had mixed emotions," Stratton admitted. "I respected the pioneering work she had done; on the other hand, when time for changes came, she was not able to deal with the changes. I had to look to the future instead of the way it was in the 1950s and 1960s. It's a whole new world."[63]

The planned merger would take place officially on January 1, 1990. The lone hurdle, of course, was the lawsuit involving control of FWBC assets. PBC held the deeds to its property and two small trust funds. The assets of the FWBC Endowment and Council represented $300,000 in cash and more than $1 million in property. Meanwhile, the ladies voted $3,000 more in scholarships to Tarrant County Junior College students.[64]

When the lawsuit was finally settled, and the parties reached a compromise, the major provisions were:

— The endowment would give the Fort Worth Boys' Club eighty-five percent of net income, of which forty percent would be operating expenses and sixty percent capital improvements and repairs,

— If ever dissolved, the assets of the endowment would go to Boys' & Girls' Club of Greater Fort Worth, Inc.,

— The council would transfer $20,000 in cash to the FWBC,

— The council would deed title to seven lots and any improvements thereon to the FWBC,

— The council would transfer to the endowment the Eagle Mountain real property and cottage,

— The council will change its name from the Fort Worth Boys' Club Council to something different.[65]

Between publication of the 1989 and 1990 yearbooks the council changed its name to Fort Worth Boys' Council, Inc. Their purpose was changed to "To support a benevolent, charitable, educational undertaking. To assist in carrying on the work of conserving the boys' life in the City of Fort Worth, Texas, and in providing opportunities for the intellectual and spiritual, the physical and social development mostly of disadvantaged boys in said community." The ladies later changed the name of their organization to Fort Worth Youth Council with plans to provide education, clothing, and fees for summer camping, for the youth of Tarrant County.[66]

When the second lawsuit began in 1989, Michael Handy, summarized the situation, saying that the controversy arose "not from any significant organizational problems among the organizations; but, rather, the problems have resulted from the fact that apparently the Boys' Club stepped rather heavily on the toes of its founder, a very elderly lady with considerable resolve."[67]

Hazel's friends knew that she had put her whole life into the boys' club. "These few people came in and took her whole life away. She should have always had *some* capacity on the board, but she was pushed away," one of her friends said. "She was heartbroken." Hazel once remarked, concerning her brother Howard, "People would not treat me this way if he had lived."[68]

Actually, Hazel could have continued her position on the board for life, for this had been voted, but she had resigned after the ladies had lost their voice and the lawsuits continued.

Hazel and the ladies of the Fort Worth Boys' Club Council had lost the fight. They continued their club for a short time, giving scholarships to young men for college, but their purpose for half a century and their assets had been circumvented. Endowment board meetings even became strained by September 1992, and some of the board resigned.[69]

✤✤✤✤✤✤✤✤✤✤✤✤✤✤✤✤✤✤✤✤✤✤✤✤✤✤✤✤✤✤✤✤✤✤✤

CHAPTER 12

Full Circle

*I*f people live long enough, they might see history repeating itself. Hazel Leigh lived that long. She saw the ladies pushed out of a boys' club again, half a century after it happened the first time. They were back to giving college scholarships and clothing to boys as their charitable endeavors. No matter that times had changed in that fifty years, that things perhaps needed to be more structured and fundraising more regular, that perhaps a ladies group would not be enough anymore. Hazel did not understand that, nor did most of her ladies.[1] Hazel lived long enough to see the FWBC merged into the PBC, the national boys' club movement become boys' and girls' clubs, and that mixture take place in Fort Worth. Because she did not agree with it, she would not accept it.

Fortunately, social events and other aspects of her life in the 1980s and 1990s were more pleasant than the clashes and confrontations involving the control of the property and assets of the FWBC Endowment and the FWBC Council. Hazel continued to receive honors and awards. When the FWBC honored her, however, the feeling persisted among the ladies that the FWBC board was only trying to make up for the bylaws reorganization and the ousting of the ladies' council. She was asked to judge a contest at an auction for the club in 1985 with the Boy of the Year Rafael Leonard so she could be introduced "as our Founder." It did not compensate for the hurt.[2] In light of United Way's pressure on FWBC to reorganize the board, it seems unusual that Hazel was making speeches for the United Way in the 1980 campaign, but she was.[3]

Sometime in the 1980s, a wealthy man from Bartlesville, Oklahoma, whom Hazel and Grover had known when they lived there, proposed to Hazel. She had kept up the friendship and visited Bartlesville frequently. He was a billionaire and said Hazel needed a chauffeur and other things, which he would be happy to provide. She agonized over the proposal but turned him down. She did not want to have someone tell her what to do; she had been independent too long.[4]

She informed the FWBC Endowment she was leaving them in her will the land and building in downtown Fort Worth which had been her father's windmill supply business, but she later changed this "due to change in FWBC, Inc. board, etc."[15]

The "boys," now men, who had remained loyal to Mrs. Leigh through the years—Darrow Hooper, Yale Lary, Bill Burklow, and others—continued their loyalty. After learning of the FWBC board action to vote the ladies' council off the board, Bill Burklow wrote Hazel: "It's hard for me to understand how the people involved in all this mess can forget what you did and mean to the FWBC—I guess it's like the old saying, 'Yeah, what have you done for me TODAY!'" He reminded her of the "many hundreds of men" who respected and loved her and told her not to let this group "get you down."[6] A former FWBC member, Larry Wayne Nelson, wrote Mrs. Leigh in 1985 and told her the things he learned "have been a part of my character my entire life—Thank you for caring."[7]

"I've lived in the little boys' world so long, I'm having a hard time adjusting to middle age now and to older people," said Hazel at age eighty-seven. She watched a little television and admitted to enjoying jazz music. "That's probably because the boys always liked loud music." About the scrapbooks she maintained, she said, "Someday, I'm going to organize all of it, maybe write a book."[8]

Even though Hazel and the ladies of the FWBC Council considered their activities completely separate from the boys' club, especially after 1983, they inadvertently created a problem with their fiftieth anniversary luncheon on March 27, 1985, at Ridglea Country Club. Fort Worth Mayor Bob Bolen proclaimed March 27, 1985, as "Mrs. Hazel Vaughn Leigh Day." Several boys' club alumni attended: Yale Lary, Pris Dominguez, Darrow Hooper, Johnny Rutherford, and Bill Burklow. In fact, Burklow wrote Mrs. Leigh the next day, "It was so exciting to me to finally meet and visit with the ladies of the Council that have contributed so much to the behind the scenes of making the FWBC the outstanding plant it is today. I know, the Council knows, that these achievements could not have come about without the loving strong leadership quality you exhibited gained from long dedicated hands on management of our club. To you, I am ever more grateful for your total commitment to that purpose."[9]

Advertisements and publicity about the FWBC Council implied that the money raised from luncheon ticket sales would go to support the boys' club—

so said the FWBC board. When some of the members of the FWBC board complained that the fiftieth anniversary luncheon was using the boys' club name to raise money but not giving it to the club, Mrs. Leigh replied that the club had celebrated its anniversary with a birthday party for the boys until about 1981 (when a new director and staff omitted it). She wrote the latter parenthetical phrase in her notes and then marked through it. "On behalf of our Ladies' Council I apologize for any mistakes that you think were made," she wrote. These handwritten comments may have been mailed or she may have only intended to send them; they are in her files.[10]

The FWBC board had kept Mrs. Leigh on the officer list as consultant but did not use her, so she resigned from that position in 1985. She knew it didn't mean anything; they were only trying to appease her. She retained her membership on the board as an honorary life member with voting privileges, however, for a little longer.[11]

Other fiftieth-year celebrations honored Hazel in 1985. She and two other ladies were initiated into the 50-Year-Club of the Woman's Club at their annual magnolia luncheon in early June 1985.[12]

About this time, Mrs. Leigh gave a telling newspaper interview. The reporter outlined Hazel's background with the boys' club and then asked her, "Would you do this again?"

"No! It's a man's job, a man's world," she said. The answer was not a spur of the moment mood or slip. Hazel wrote the same comments out in longhand two or three times in her papers.[13]

The FWBC and the Child Study Center celebrated the second annual National Philanthropy Day on November 14, 1987. The special day was the creation of the National Society of Fund Raising Executives. At a banquet at River Crest Country Club, Hazel was honored for a "Lifetime of Philanthropy," and W. A. Landreth, Sr., was honored as "Philanthropist of the Year."[14]

In May 1988, at age ninety, Hazel attended the annual national BCA conference in Orlando, Florida, made every session, and sat on the front row, ready to listen when each program started. She made the rounds of dinners, social functions, and special activities. A younger friend, Barbara Wheeler, a member of the FWBC Council, frequently traveled with Hazel to out-of-town functions like the BCA annual convention. Obviously, Hazel's purpose for being there was not the same as it had been in 1939—to learn how to run a boys' club.

*Hazel in her nineties. Courtesy
Fort Worth Public Library.*

She attended to see the friends she had made, to have some place to go, and probably, to prove to folks that she was still around and active.

That fall the ladies' were assisting five young men in college. They bought 500 pairs of shoes for small boys to start school. One of Hazel's ladies commented that in some ways Hazel had not realized that times had changed. Perhaps shoes for little boys were not needed as much as they had been fifty years earlier.[15]

As the local boys clubs were preparing to merge and follow the national trend, Joe Cordova came to Fort Worth in 1989 as executive director of PBC, replacing Michie Brous. Cordova, who previously had worked with boys' clubs in Waco and Farmington, New Mexico, came in with the understanding that he would head the combined organizations. At that time, PBC oversaw the East Side and Burleson clubs, and FWBC controlled the Eagle Mountain unit. The White Settlement club had temporarily closed.[16]

Hazel kept up her correspondence with friends she had met in the national organization. Bill Hinckley of the Omaha Boys' Clubs wrote that he wasn't happy about the merger with the girls either. Because Hazel and the ladies' council were not supporting the FWBC financially anymore, Hinckley urged them to donate money to a national museum of the boys' club movement. Nothing in the records suggests that they did.[17]

Hazel knew that many in the nationwide boys' club movement agreed with her that girls did not belong in the club. You couldn't solve all the problems of the boys' home situations, poverty, ethnic differences, etc., and then add girls to the mix too.[18]

Shortly after the local merger was accomplished, the new board launched a capital improvement campaign. They hired professional fund raisers and raised $4.2 million for a new FWBC Northside building (completed in 1995), an East Side building (1994), and a Panther Boys' Club building (1995), and new administrative offices (1994). The name Fort Worth Boys' Club was dropped, and the new facility at 2000 Ellis was simply called the Northside branch. PBC kept its name, however. Joe Cordova explained that one reason for the capital campaign and all of the rebuilding was to redesign clubs with facilities (restrooms, showers, etc.) for both boys and girls. He agreed that incorporating girls into the movement made it harder to get boys to focus on what really was needed for them. He had not wanted the girls added either.[19]

The difference in attitude among the executive directors who did not want girls and Hazel's attitude was that the men—often considering their own livelihoods—faced the reality of what was happening nationwide. Hazel would not.

The Boys' Club Professional Association changed its name to Association of Boys' and Girls' Club Professionals in the summer of 1990. Hazel still was a member, so she received the renamed magazine, *Profiles.*[20]

If Hazel saw any printed information on the makeup of the new board of the Boys' and Girls' Clubs of Greater Fort Worth it would be like her to count the number of women on the board. Out of forty-two members of the executive committee and directors in 1993, only seven were women.[21]

Only a couple of years after Hazel's death, the Boys' and Girls' Clubs of Greater Fort Worth consisted of seven clubs: Panther, Northside (formerly FWBC), East Side, J. A. Cavile, Butler Branch, Washington Heights, and Van Zandt-Guinn. A total of 130 employees served the seven clubs and the administrative offices. Of a maximum of fifty board members, in 1997 eleven were women. The total budget per year was $3.5 million with only twenty-eight percent coming from the United Way.[22]

Meanwhile, Hazel's life did go on without direct involvement in the FWBC. By the 1990s she was saying, "I have to get younger friends; all of my friends are dying." In fact, she continued to feel and act younger than her chronological age because of her activity and younger friends. Once when the FWBC Council meeting was at Gloria Davis's house, Hazel told her, "Station someone at the front door for the little old ladies on a stick." Then she stopped and realized, "Oh, I forget that I'm one!"[23]

Wealthy ladies still came to the socials. Through the years Hazel always instigated them. "You have a nice big house. Let's have some meetings at your house," Hazel would tell one of her wealthy friends, and the ladies would meet there for a tea.[24]

As Hazel got older she received enough retirement money to live in style in her Hulen Street apartment. Several years earlier she had contributed money to an annuity benefiting the United Way, which was set up on an estimate of how long she would live. It had projected so much money per month until age eighty-seven but would keep paying if she lived longer. Later when she was well past that age she used to laugh and say, "I fooled them." She was amused that it was United Way money.[25]

When Hazel needed help, she called one of her ladies or one of her former "boys." Buddy Carter, a former FWBC member and then a member of the FWBC Endowment board, was in the real estate business on Fort Worth's West Side, near Hazel's apartment. She called him when her garbage disposal would not work. Carter went by and cleared it for her. She commented to him that, at age ninety-two, she had just renewed her driver license for four more years! Carter believed that she looked a dozen years younger than that age.[26]

Hazel thus remained in good health into her mid-nineties, but she admitted to Fran Chiles, wife of Eddie Chiles—once owner of the Western Company and the Texas Rangers—that arthritis in her hands made writing difficult for her.[27]

When she attended a luncheon and reception in the Camellia I Room of the Fort Worth Club in September 1990, she was already ninety-three. She helped greet two women from the United Kingdom who were on a philanthropy fact-finding mission. Of course, the club ladies introduced Hazel and were proud of her.[28]

Probably because of Hazel's youthful acquaintance with Fort Worth society figures and then with the wives of oil executives and others on the council, she was listed for many years along with Fort Worth's elite in the *Fort Worth Social Directory* each time it appeared. This continued until her death, and the directory immediately following called attention to her accomplishments.[29]

Mrs. Leigh remained active in both the ladies' FWBC Council and the Endowment Fund board in the early 1990s, but both groups began to meet less frequently. Sometimes the executive councils would meet at her apartment on Hulen, at separate times, for her convenience. Soon, however, the ladies group began to fizzle out because the ladies got tired of hearing about how the FWBC board had voted them out. Tensions broke up the endowment board as well.[30]

Some of the last official activities of the council involved changing its name, as the court settlement directed. The council held five regular meetings that year, with Mrs. Tom Manuel serving as president. She signed an agreement on June 14, 1991, by which the council sold the seven lots they owned (on which the FWBC facilities sat) to the FWBC Endowment Fund for $10. The property would be used by the Boys' and Girls' Clubs of Greater Fort Worth, Inc. The 1991 agreement also stipulated that forty percent of the income from the endowment could be used for general operating expenses of the Boys' and Girls' Clubs, and sixty percent for capital improvements and repairs. The last *Yearbook* for the FWBC Council (renamed Fort Worth Youth Council) was published in 1991.[31]

At different times, various men on the endowment board had been asked to serve as executor of Hazel's considerable estate—most of which would have gone to the boys' club, had the ousting of the ladies' group and lawsuit never taken place. When Hazel felt her executor no longer agreed with her on boys' club issues, she asked someone else to take the job. Hazel had no close family, only distant cousins. Preston Geren, Jr., took on the responsibility for Hazel at the last. Important ladies in his life had been on the ladies' council, and he felt he was the only one left to help Hazel.[32]

Fortunately, in Hazel's later years Vaughn family members and loyal friends invited her to Thanksgiving and Christmas dinners. She and longtime traveling friend Barbara Wheeler met for lunch and attended bazaars and dinners at

St. Andrews Episcopal, and Barbara often took Hazel shopping. Once when they went to San Francisco, Hazel and Barbara took a taxi to the area where she and Grover had lived.[33]

Hazel attended the '93 club functions at the Woman's Club and played bridge once a week. She drove her own late-model Cadillac until the last two or three years of her life. When the car was damaged in an accident, she bought a new one. After Preston Geren, Jr., became her executor, he persuaded her to sell her car.[34]

One of her loyal friends, Eileen Snyder, took Hazel to the doctor, who happened to be Eileen's husband Dr. Roy Snyder. He served as Hazel's doctor for about fifteen years. "Hazel wouldn't use her Medicare Card. She paid for the visits to the doctor's office herself," Eileen explained.[35]

The Fort Worth Commission on the Status of Women honored Mrs. Leigh as one of twelve "Outstanding Women of the Year" with their special "Pioneer Award" at an annual reception March 25, 1992, at Round-Up Inn in the Will Rogers Memorial Complex. Mayor Kay Granger was another of the honorees. Ken Hopkins, senior librarian for the Fort Worth Public Library's genealogy and local history section, took Hazel to the evening reception. She had been consulting him about the disposition of records from the FWBC, FWBC Council and FWBC Endowment Fund.[36]

Disappointments as well as honors came to Hazel in her last years. Her father's building at 715 West Belknap was torn down to make room for a parking lot. An historical marker was suggested, but the building had already been torn down by June 1992. Another event she was probably not too pleased to read about was the 1992 election of Lyn Downing as president of the board of directors of the Boys' and Girls' Clubs of Greater Fort Worth. Downing had been one of the community-at-large women who helped vote the FWBC Council off the FWBC board in 1983.[37]

More heartache came when she learned that the Eagle Mountain Boys' Club shut down for lack of funds. The United Way had never given operating funds, so the Azle community and the FWBC had to allocate money. Later the Boys' and Girls' Clubs of Greater Fort Worth did as well, but it finally proved too difficult. Preston Geren remembered how terribly disappointed Hazel was when she heard of its closing.[38]

The beginning of 1993 brought another frustration. In February she was trying to recover the assets of the B. F. Weekley estate, which had been donated to the endowment for the purpose of capital improvement, especially the building at Eagle Mountain. Shortly after Hazel attended the annual meeting of the Boys' and Girls' Clubs of Greater Fort Worth in February, she received a letter from Joe Cordova, asking when the clubs would receive the allocation (interest) from the endowment that they were to receive each year according to the settlement. He also told her that the board wanted to know how the funds were invested.[39]

Hazel continued to live at the Hulen address for a year after Geren persuaded her to sell her car. After Hazel fell a few times, once even requiring stitches on her head, Geren persuaded her to move to the Trinity Terrace retirement apartments at 1400 Texas Street on the west edge of downtown. He had tried to persuade her to move to El Paso to be near her cousin Vera Martin Duncan's children, but she would not. She moved on March 10 into apartments 708 and 709 at Trinity Terrace; she combined the two apartments into one because she needed plenty of room for her furniture and antiques.[40]

After the move, Geren's secretary, Judy Wilson, would pick Hazel up and take her to the beauty shop, the bank, or to lunch. Sometimes they had lunch at the City Club. Hazel always dressed primly and properly, with gloves, high heels, and usually dark glasses because of her drooping eye—which still bothered her. She carried herself with straight, youthful posture. Hazel's health had always been good, but during the last two years or so her blood pressure rose, and she had some stomach problems.[41]

Awards and recognition continued to come, perhaps partly because she had lived so long. On April 29, 1993, the North Fort Worth Historical Society presented Hazel with their Tad Lucas Life Achievement Award at a dinner held in the open-air Stockyards Station. The audience gave her a standing ovation.[42] "I never thought I'd live so long to see North Fort Worth have such a beautiful place to be as down here," she said.[43]

Preston Geren became concerned that if Mrs. Leigh died before some resolution was reached concerning the endowment fund and the FWBC Council accounts, it would take a lawsuit to resolve the disposition of the funds. She kept promising to meet with the endowment and the council boards but procrastinated. Finally the boards met without her. Geren had his secretary write a letter, dated September 1, 1993, for Hazel to sign, effectively resigning her position on the boards. He called the boards to meet at the Camp Bowie

Hazel in her nineties with her antiques and memorabilia, keeping scrapbooks for the book she always intended to write someday. Courtesy Fort Worth Public Library.

National Bank. There, after a vote, they transferred the funds to the Boys' and Girls' Clubs of Greater Fort Worth. Hazel was not told. Joe Cordova explained that an endowment was created as the Hazel Vaughn Leigh Endowment that could not be touched; only the interest could be used. The endowment was worth about $800,000, because money from the 1995 sale of the Eagle Mountain property was added to it.[44]

Hazel mentioned to some people that she planned to start a book in January 1994. She wanted to tell her side of the controversy with the FWBC board. But by mid-1994, Hazel had to have nurses around the clock at Trinity Terrace. The nurses reported a pleasant ninety-one-pound lady whose goal was to gain up to 100 pounds. She talked about the boys' club a lot to her nurses. Just three weeks before her death, she was still getting up, getting dressed, going for a walk in the hall, and eating at her own dining table in her apartment.[45]

Hazel died April 27, 1995, and was buried at Greenwood Cemetery. The Reverend Bert Honea from St. Andrews Episcopal officiated. Some of the men who grew up attending the boys' club served as pall bearers.[46]

Hazel had made a new will a couple of years before she died. Although she had always said she would leave all her money to the boys' club, she changed her mind because she was dissatisfied with the way it was being run, the merging of the clubs, the addition of the girls, and because she felt pushed aside.[47] "It's hard, I tell you. It's just hard staying out of things," she commented toward the last. "I'm giving my things to the library because the kids today don't read like they did back then. My boys, even though they loved to box and play ball, had to be able to read. We made sure there were books around, and we always taught them to read."[48]

In her will she requested that a history of the "Boys' Clubs in Tarrant County, Texas and their founders" be written. She wanted the 'long story' told, Geren explained, so people could 'compare the future with what she did in the past.'[49] As the FWBC attorney wrote in one of his depositions during the lawsuit and subsequent settlement, Hazel Vaughn Leigh was a lady "with considerable resolve."

Epilogue

Those who believed that Mrs. Leigh became too possessive of the Fort Worth Boys' Club might understand her attitude better if they compared her with other "founders." In Odessa, Texas, Marjorie Morris led the drive to raise funds for a Globe Theatre, a replica of William Shakespeare's original theater. Not only did she begin that effort in the 1940s, she later raised funds, planned activities and nudged people to contribute until a replica of the cottage belonging to Anne Hathaway, Shakespeare's wife, also stood on the grounds. It was designed to be used as a library. Mrs. Morris, a strong Baptist, handpicked people to serve on the board, dictated the policy that "God's name will not be taken in vain" in performances at the Globe, and generally dominated the project for fifty years. Only when she was in her late eighties and having health problems did she slow down. She too did not want to give up her "hands on" control to others. Like Hazel, she had no children of her own and outlived by many years a husband who was an alcoholic.[1]

In a similar manner, the well-known Jane Addams, who started Hull House in Chicago, demonstrated traits quite like Hazel Leigh's. Hull House was "her" settlement house (it also had a boys' club). Hull House opened in 1889 to serve the immigrant poor in Chicago's factory and stockyards district. Jane Addams was "almost a genius at raising money." But she did not prepare for the day when the settlement house would have to operate without her. When she died in 1935, others carried on. When Hazel visited Hull House, she noted that the crafts and programs were similar to those at the FWBC. [2]

Hazel can also be compared to Edward Joseph Flanagan, the "Father Flanagan" of Boys' Town, west of Omaha, Nebraska. His life work began in December 1917 when the juvenile court placed five boys in his care. Flanagan's at first had a home or shelter near the Omaha stockyards, just as Hull House and the FWBC were near the stockyards and meat-packing plants in their cities. Stockyards areas attracted immigrant families who earned low wages and whose children were often left unattended while both parents worked.[3]

Even in Fort Worth, another woman saw her name and efforts attached to a charitable cause. In 1910 Edna Gladney became director of the Texas Children's Home and Aid Society, chartered six years earlier. In 1927 she was named superintendent. A 1941 movie, "Blossoms in the Dust," dramatized her work with unwed mothers. The adoption agency and home for unwed mothers which she directed for so many years was renamed the Edna Gladney Home in 1950.[4]

One person identifying his or her life work with one project and being possessive about that project or cause is not unusual. A United Way volunteer, William Sarsgard, explained that agencies created and dominated by one person worry United Way because of the issue of permanence. The FWBC board was not the only local example that concerned them. Many other organizations had no provisions for board rotation, attendance, or even regular monthly meetings. Boards needed to be organized in the manner United Way began to require for purposes of continuity. The function of United Way, according to Sarsgard, was to bring these agencies into the twentieth century in terms of board operation. A founder who also served as executive of an agency or was on the board was a red flag to United Way, he said. That, of course, was Hazel's role for forty years.[5]

Hazel's friends, the frustrated ladies of the council, and even her critics, agreed that Hazel truly cared about the boys and was dedicated to them. Her positive points far outweighed the negative. There are men who as boys would have starved had it not been for the FWBC. Regardless of her dictatorial ways, "her benevolence overshadowed all. She saved many a young man."[6]

Is there a villain in the story? Not really. The FWBC board members who became convinced the council representatives had to be replaced and the board enlarged were forced to take that stand by United Way. Jim Stratton of BCA called Paul Koeppe and Trey Shannon "fine men" and "real change agents." Some ladies who were close to Hazel and remain saddened and bitter about the way she was treated did not know about the pressure from United Way and the national boys' club organization.[7]

Despite her opposition to opening clubs to girls, Hazel was well respected in the national movement. "When she spoke, she knew what she was talking about," said Jim Caufield, a senior vice president with Boys' and Girls' Clubs of America.[8]

What remains unique about FWBC is that volunteer community efforts worked so well for so long. Society women on the council and dedicated business leaders from Kiwanis took a hands-on approach. They knew many of the boys personally, and they appeared at regular intervals to host Easter egg hunts, watermelon parties, Halloween apple-dunkings, and the annual Christmas party. They saw the freckles of twelve-year-old Snooky Pressley, the wide-eyed excitement of seven-year-old Billy Burklow, the serious leadership of fifteen-year-old Otis Snow, and they heard the accordion music of Johnny Kohut.

Many people could write out a check today to the Boys' and Girls' Club of Greater Fort Worth or the United Way, but that would probably not bring the same satisfaction that came to the people who supported FWBC in the first half-century of its existence.

The boys' club on the North Side and the $800,000 "Hazel Vaughn Leigh Endowment" with the Boys' and Girls' Clubs of Greater Fort Worth remain testimony to the energetic endeavors of Hazel Vaughn Leigh.

Notes

Chapter 1

1. Nurses' Log of HVL care, July 27, 1994. In possession of author.

2. Nurses' Log, July 17 and Aug. 3, 1994.

3. Joanne Pettit, Interviewer, Oral Histories of Fort Worth, Inc., July 22, 1977, "Hazel Vaughn Leigh," p. 5. Sponsored by Junior League, HVL Collection, Fort Worth Public Library.

4. Nelda Gregor, interview by author, Fort Worth, Dec. 9, 1997.

5. Oral History, "Hazel Vaughn Leigh," p. 21.

6. "Biographical Notes" in History Box No. 1, HVL Papers, Fort Worth Public Library. Also Lila Bunch Race, *Pioneer Fort Worth, Texas: Life, Times and Families of South Tarrant County,* pp. 32–33.

7. Race, *Pioneer Fort Worth, Texas,* p. 99.

8. Copy of Certificate of Birth, Hazel Elizabeth Vaughn, Fort Worth, Tarrant County, Texas, in HVL Collection, FWPL. Also Photo of Samuel and Nancy Elizabeth Vaughn's Grandchildren in Photo Box 3, HVL Collection. Also Oral History, "Hazel Vaughn Leigh," pp. 6, 15–16.

9. Oral History, "Hazel Vaughn Leigh," p. 6.

10. Roze McCoy Porter, *Thistle Hill: The Cattle Baron's Legacy,* p. 86.

11. Beverly Fogle, one of the nurses who stayed with Mrs. Leigh at Trinity Terrace, telephone interview by author, July 27, 1998. Also J'Nell L. Pate, *North of the River: A Brief History of North Fort Worth,* pp. 109–12.

12. Photo of Hazel Vaughn about age seven or eight in Photo Box 3, HVL Collection, FWPL.

13. Two photos of children, DeZavala School, 1905, Photo Box 3, HVL Collection, FWPL.

14. Betty Duncan, distant cousin of HVL, telephone interview by author, Aug. 2, 1997.

15. Obituary in Sam Vaughn Clippings Folder, History Box 2, HVL Collection, FWPL.

16. Christopher Evans, "Personalities For the Boys," *Fort Worth Star-Telegram,* May 31, 1992, section E, p. 5.

17. Funeral Book, History Box 2, HVL Collection, FWPL, and Race, *Pioneer Fort Worth, Texas,* p. 100.

18. Oral History, "Hazel Vaughn Leigh," p. 3; and Photo of College Avenue Baptist Church Sunday School, 1910, in Photo Box 3, HVL Collection, FWPL.

19. Photo of Sam Vaughn, Sr., and Elizabeth Vaughn (Hazel's grandparents) and his brother Freeman Vaughn and Mrs. Freeman Vaughn, note on back of photo, Photo Box 3, HVL Collection, FWPL; also Oral History, "Hazel Vaughn Leigh," p. 21.

20. Ruby Kerr, telephone interview by author, Feb. 23, 1998. Also "Biographic Notes" in History Box 1, and Oral Interview, "Hazel Vaughn Leigh," pp. 1–2.

21. Nancy Duncan Jenkins, second cousin of HVL and daughter of Vera Martin Duncan, telephone interview by author, Aug. 2, 1997. Also Vera Martin Photo, 1912, El Paso, in Photo Box 1, HVL Collection, FWPL. Because Mrs. Jenkins knows that her parents married in January 1912, Hazel must have spent the summer of 1911 in El Paso rather than 1912 as she marked on her photo.

CHAPTER 2

1. Dance Card of Hazel Vaughn for Banquet and Reception given in honor of the Fort Worth High School Football Team, Westbrook Hotel, Dec. 8, 1913, in Photo Box 2, HVL Collection, Fort Worth Public Library. This was Central High School, which sometimes was called Fort Worth High School.

2. 1914 Annual Central High School, Paschal High School Library, Fort Worth. Also Gregor interview.

3. Nurses Log, Aug. 16, 1994; also TCU Annual, *The Horned Frog,* 1918, Vol. XIV, Graduates Section, no pages cited.

4. TCU Annual, Vol. XV [misnumbered, should be XII], *The Horned Frog,* 1916, football section, unnumbered pages; and TCU Annual, Vol. XIV, *The Horned Frog,* 1918, graduation section, unnumbered pages.

5. Oral History, "Hazel Vaughn Leigh," p. 3.

6. Ibid., p. 4.

7. Ibid., p. 16.

8. Porter, *Thistle Hill: The Cattle Baron's Legacy,* p. 337; also *Fort Worth Social Directory,* p. 205.

9. Oral History, "Hazel Vaughn Leigh," p. 4; and J'Nell L. Pate, *Livestock Legacy: The Fort Worth Stockyards, 1887-1987,* p. 62.

10. "Family Life Folder," in History Box 1, HVL Collection, FWPL.

11. Clay Reynolds, *A Hundred Years of Heroes: A History of the Southwestern Exposition and Livestock Show,* pp. 102, 104.

12. "Family Life Folder," History Box 1, HVL Collection, FWPL.

13. Ibid.

14. Ibid.

15. Leonard Sanders and Ronnie C. Tyler, *How Fort Worth Became the Texasmost City,* p. 84; and Oral History, "Hazel Vaughn Leigh," pp. 16, 3.

16. Oral History, "Hazel Vaughn Leigh," p. 18.

17. Howard Vaughn, Military Record, in History Box 2, HVL Collection, FWPL; also Photo of Howard Vaughn and information on back, Photo Box 3, HVL Collection.

18. Sanders and Tyler, *How Fort Worth Became the Texasmost City,* p. 169.

19. Oral History, "Hazel Vaughn Leigh," p. 18.

20. Oral History, "Hazel Vaughn Leigh," p. 18; and "Biographical Notes," History Box 1, HVL Collection, FWPL. Also William E. Jary, Jr., *Camp Bowie, Fort Worth: 1917-18,* p. 7.

21. Text of Radio Interview on Community Chest Program, Jan. 22, 1941, Harold Barnes, Interviewing, p. 2, in "Historical Notes" folder, History Box 1, HVL Collection, FWPL.

22. Lewis L. Gould, ed., *The Progressive Era,* p. 13.

23. "Woman Founder of Boys Club Will Get Degree at 46," *Fort Worth Star-Telegram,* May 21, 1944, "Hazel Vaughn Leigh," *Fort Worth Star-Telegram* Clipping File, UTA Special Collections. Also Ruby Schmidt, *Fort Worth and Tarrant County: A Historical Guide,* p. 47.

CHAPTER 3

1. Oliver Knight, *Fort Worth: Outpost on the Trinity,* p. 190. Also Caleb Pirtle, III, *Fort Worth: The Civilized West,* pp. 114–15.

2. *Oil Legends of Fort Worth,* the Historical Committee of The Fort Worth Petroleum Club, pp. 74, 441. Also, Knight, *Fort Worth: Outpost on the Trinity,* p. 192.

3. Grover Leigh Funeral Book, loose paper in History Book 2, HVL Collection, FWPL.

4. Military Record of Grover Cleveland Leigh in History Box 2, HVL Collection, FWPL.

5. Margaret Withers Teague, *History of Washington County and Surrounding Areas,* pp. 56, 58, 63, 335.

6. Harold F. Williamson, Ralph L. Andreano, Arnold R. Daum, and Gilbert C. Klose, *The American Petroleum Industry: The Age of Energy, 1899–1959*, pp. 350–51; also Diana Olien, telephone interview by author, Apr. 2, 1998; and *Oil Legends of Fort Worth*, p. 277.

7. Wedding Announcement of Hazel and Grover, Photo Box 3, HVL Collection, FWPL.

8. Clipping, *Fort Worth Star-Telegram*, Sun., Apr. 29, 1923, in black scrapbook, HVL Collection, FWPL.

9. Information on back of photo of Grover Leigh in Photo Box 3, HVL Collection, FWPL. Letterhead of the stationery was The Empire Companies, Bartlesville, Okla.

10. Gregor interview.

11. William Issel and Robert W. Cherney, *San Francisco 1865–1932: Politics, Power and Urban Development*, pp. 190–91; also from a 1920s map of downtown San Francisco supplied by the reference librarian, San Francisco Public Library.

12. Issel and Cherney, *San Francisco*, pp. 63, 76, and photo section between pp. 112–13; also Jerry Flamm, *Good Life in Hard Times*, p. 4.

13. Susie Ryan Phipps, "Boys' Club Founder Recalls Rough Start," *The News-Tribune*, Oct. 7, 1977, p. 25.

14. Gregor interview.

15. "History Notes," Fort Worth Boys' Club folder in History Box 1, HVL Collection, FWPL.

16. List of dates of National Boys' Clubs in "Hazel Vaughn Leigh" Box in HVL Collection, FWPL. Also James M. Hamill, *The Major And His Boys: The Story of Major Sidney Peixotto and the Columbia Park Boys' Club*, pp. 10–11, 16.

17. Hamill, *The Major and His Boys*, pp. 5, 17–18. The club still exists in San Francisco.

18. *Oil Legends of Fort Worth*, p. 65; and Janet Schmelzer, *Where the West Begins: Fort Worth and Tarrant County*, p. 217; and Williamson, et al., *The American Petroleum Industry*, p. 550.

19. *Oil Legends of Fort Worth*, pp. 42, 59, 121.

20. Olien interview; and *Oil Legends of Fort Worth*, p. 168.

21. *Oil Legends of Fort Worth*, pp. 123, 200.

22. "Iowa Visitor Here Honored At Pretty Bridge Luncheon," *The Fort Worth Press*, Jan. 1928, p. 6.

23. Box of Clippings dated 1940–1969 (but with many earlier than that), HVL Collection, FWPL.

24. *Fort Worth City Directory,* 1926, p. 573; 1927, p. 587; 1928, p. 601.

25. Clipping, "Train Costs Life of Grover Leigh," in "Grover Leigh" folder in History Boxes 1 and 2, HVL Collection, FWPL.

26. Walter B. Scott, letter to Grover Leigh, May 29, 1932, in HVL Collection, FWPL.

27. Jerry Flemmons, *Amon: The Life of Amon Carter, Sr., of Texas,* pp. 78, 486. They divorced in 1941.

28. Oral History, "Hazel Vaughn Leigh," p. 17; and Amon G. Carter, letter to Grover Leigh, July 30, 1929, in HVL Collection, FWPL.

29. Pirtle, *Fort Worth: The Civilized West,* pp. 125, 129; Jerry Flemmons, "Amon: The Man Who Invented the Cowboy," manuscript, pp. 207, 210; and Sister Mary Ailbe Keaveney, "The Depression Era in Fort Worth, Texas 1929–1934," MA Thesis, University of Texas at Austin, 1974, pp. 59–60.

30. Pate, *Livestock Legacy,* p. 157; and Keaveney, "The Depression Era in Fort Worth," p. 65.

31. History Box 2, HVL Collection, FWPL.

32. Church Office Records, St. Andrews Episcopal Church; also "Education, TCU" folder in History Box 1, HVL Collection, FWPL.

33. "Takes Office as Chief Deputy United States Marshal," *Dallas Journal,* Nov. 17, 1933, clipping in History Box 2, HVL Collection, FWPL.

34. Oral Interview, "Hazel Vaughn Leigh," p. 16.

35. Program of Dances, Photo Box 2, Grover Leigh in HVL Collection, FWPL.

36. Gregor interview.

CHAPTER 4

1. R. K. Atkinson, *The Boys' Club,* pp. 22–23.

2. Ibid., p. 22; also William Edwin Hall, *100 Years and Millions of Boys: The Dynamic Story of the Boys' Clubs of America,* pp. 7–8.

3. "Historical Notes" Folder, History Box 1, HVL Collection, FWPL.

4. Pamphlet, "Member Organizations of the Boys' Clubs of America," 1946, p. 46; also "Boys & Girls' Clubs of Greater Dallas: A History of Service, 1965–1998," one page sheet sent to author. By the late 1990s, ten clubs existed in Dallas with a Maple Avenue Club, a Richardson Club and a Cedar Springs Club. In 1990 the organization's name was changed to Boys' and Girls' Clubs of Greater Dallas.

5. "Public Welfare," *Fort Worth Press,* Feb. 5, 1926, in Federal Writers' Project, *Research Data,* Vol. 29, pp. 11207–208.

6. Copy of *Rotograph* Fort Worth in black scrapbook, 1928–1934 Panther Boys' Club Clipping in HVL Collection, FWPL. Also "Public Welfare," *Fort Worth Press,* in *Research Data,* pp. 11207–208; and "Newsies First To Sign Up in Panther Club," *Fort Worth Star-Telegram,* Oct. 30, 1949, morning edition, *Fort Worth Star-Telegram* Clippings "Panther Boys' Club," UTA Special Collections.

7. Panther Boys' Club Gold Bond in Correspondence Box 2, HVL Collection, FWPL; *Research Data,* no headline, Vol. 58, p. 22977. Also Mack Williams, "In Old Fort Worth," "L. B. Price Gave His Life to Start Panther Boys' Club," *Fort Worth News-Tribune,* Dec. 19, 1986, p. 8B; and "$36,000 Fund For Boys Aim of Rotarians," *Fort Worth Star-Telegram,* June 28, 1947, morning edition, *Fort Worth Star-Telegram* Clippings, UTA Special Collections. Other officers besides Slay, president, were Allison, vice president; Ellison Harding, treasurer, and Ickes as secretary. Notes from PBC Women's Council, 1927, in BCA Box, HVL Collection, FWPL.

8. "Panther and Fort Worth Boys' Clubs To Merge," *The Eagle Extra,* Dec. 1, 1989, p. 6.

9. "Newsies First To Sign Up in Panther Club," *Fort Worth Star-Telegram,* Oct. 30, 1949, morning edition, FWST Clippings, "Panther Boys' Club," UTA Special Collections; "Panther Boys' Club" in *Research Data,* Vol. 77, p. 30496. Many years later Myrtle Dockery Bryenton gave $300,000 to the Fort Worth Boys' Club Endowment Fund, Inc., in her will; see page four of four-page handwritten history of PBC in BCA Box, HVL Collection, FWPL. Also Martha Justice to F. J. Keller, May 14, 1945, and attached history of PBC, Martha Justice Ball Collection, FWPL.

10. Graham Ball, husband of Martha Justice Ball, telephone interview by author, Sept. 30, 1997. Martha worked at Panther Boys' Club from 1926 to 1947. Wanda Gibson, niece of Martha Justice Ball, interview by author, Fort Worth, Aug. 4, 1998; and Nadeane Walker, "Big Sister to the Panther Boys' Says They Have (but Are Not) Problems," *Fort Worth Star-Telegram,* Sun., May 2, 1943, p. 4.

11. Notes from PBC Women's Council 1927, in BCA Box, HVL Collection, FWPL. The marriage did not last. Anne would marry three more times, the last marriage to Charles Tandy. Scrapbook Clippings: "Mrs. Waggoner to Head Council," *Record-Telegram,* May 20, 1927; "Auxiliary to Panther Club Selects Officers," *Record-Telegram,* Jan. 25, 1927; and "Women Organize Boys' Club Group," *Record-Telegram,* Jan. 10, 1927. Also untitled, handwritten page in "Historical Notes" Folder in History Box 1, HVL Collection, FWPL.

12. "Panther Boys' Club" in *Research Data,* Vol. 77, p. 30498; "Boyville Gardens at Lake Worth Is New Corporation of Panther Club," *Fort Worth*

Star-Telegram, Sun., Mar. 25, 1928, and "Panther Boys' Camp Is Alive," *Fort Worth Press,* May 17, 1929, both in black scrapbook, Panther Boys' Club Clippings in HVL Collection, FWPL.

13. "Public Welfare," *Fort Worth Press,* June 14, 1928, in *Research Data,* Vol. 29, p. 11235; Also "Manages Review for Boys' Fund," *Record,* June 1, 1928, in black scrapbook, PBC, in HVL Collection, FWPL.

14. K. S. Ickes, superintendent, letter to members, Jan. 22, 1929, in black scrapbook, PBC, HVL Collection, FWPL.

15. "Panther Boys' Club Officers Are Named," *Fort Worth Press,* June 12, 1930, in black scrapbook, PBC, in HVL Collection, FWPL. Also Open Membership Letter, Oct. 13, 1931, for 1931–32 year in Minutes Box, PBC, HVL Collection. Also Letter Invitation from K. S. Ickes, Exec. Sec., Oct. 22, 1931, 4 to 6 P.M. at Mrs. J. C. Maxwell's in black scrapbook, HVL Collection. Also "Committee for Benefit Tea Named," *Fort Worth Press,* May 23, 1932, in black scrapbook; and Women's Council Minutes, May 6 and Oct. 15, 1932, in Minutes, Panther, HVL Collection, FWPL.

16. "Do You Know," *Fort Worth Press,* Dec. 7, 1932, in black scrapbook, PBC, HVL Collection, FWPL.

17. Pauline Naylor, "Council for Boys' Club Active," *Fort Worth Star-Telegram,* Sun., June 18, 1933, in black scrapbook, PBC, HVL Collection, FWPL.

18. Article in *Morning Star-Telegram,* Mar. 21, 1933, in black scrapbook, PBC, HVL Collection, FWPL. The PBC and the YMCA did not merge, but in 1990 an important merger of clubs would take place.

19. *Fort Worth Morning Star-Telegram,* July 30, 1933, p. 4, as cited in Keaveney, "The Depression Era in Fort Worth, Texas, 1929–1934," p. 131.

20. Minutes, PBC Women's Council, Oct. 9, 1933, HVL Collection, FWPL.

21. Minutes, PBC Women's Council, Nov. 13, 1933; and Minutes, PBC Women's Council, Dec. 11, 1933, HVL Collection, FWPL.

22. Pauline Naylor, "Women's Council of Boys' Club Busy Now," *Fort Worth Star-Telegram,* May 20, 1934, black scrapbook, HVL Collection, FWPL.

23. Pirtle, *Fort Worth: The Civilized West,* p. 499; also Robert H. Talbert, *Cowtown Metropolis: Case Study of a City's Growth and Structure,* p. 211; and "Fort Worth Community Chest and 27 Allied Agencies," *Research Data,* Vol. 54, p. 21552.

24. Clipping, "Women Plan Chest Crusade," 1934 [no month, day], in Box of Clippings, HVL Collection, FWPL.

25. U.S. Bureau of the Census, *Fifteenth Census of the United States: 1930,* Unemployment, I, 952, as cited in Donald Alvin Henderson, "Fort Worth

and the Depression 1929–1933," MA Thesis, TCU, 1964, pp. 82, 34; also Keaveney, "The Depression Era in Fort Worth," p. 46.

26. Henderson, "Fort Worth and the Depression," pp. 49, 51.

27. Ibid., pp. 64, 67; Fort Worth Record-Telegram, Jan. 7, 1930, p. 4, as cited in Keaveney, "The Depression Era," pp. 38, 87, 89–90, 111.

28. Fort Worth Star-Telegram, Sept. 9, 1931, p. 6, as cited in Henderson, p. 73; Fort Worth Star-Telegram, Jan. 25, 1932, p. 1, as cited in Henderson, p. 62.

29. Fort Worth Star-Telegram, Mar. 3, 1932, p. 3, as cited in Henderson, p. 79; Fort Worth Star-Telegram, Dec. 16, 1932, morning edition, p. 8, as cited in Keaveney, "The Depression Era," p. 110.

30. Keaveney, "The Depression Era," pp. 123, 141.

31. List on back of Mrs. Grover C. Leigh, letter to Board of Directors, Panther Boys' Club (1934), Hazel Vaughn Leigh Box, HVL Collection, FWPL. Also Clipping, "2 Benefit Parties Planned to Buy Equipment for Boys' Camp," in Hazel Vaughn Leigh Box, HVL Collection, FWPL; untitled clipping, Ibid.; and Pauline Naylor, "Women's Council of Boys' Club Busy Now," May 20, 1934, Fort Worth Star-Telegram, in Ibid.

32. Minutes, PBC Women's Council meeting, Nov. 26, 1934; Minutes PBC Women's Council meeting, Dec. 10, 1934.

CHAPTER 5

1. Minutes, PBC Women's Council, June 11, 1934, HVL Collection, FWPL.

2. 1934 Yearbook of the Boys' Clubs of America, Inc., p. 34.

3. "The History of the Beginning of Why the Fort Worth Boys' Club was Organized by the Ladies," two handwritten pages, Hazel Vaughn Leigh Box, HVL Collection, FWPL.

4. Minutes, Panther Boys' Club, Sept. 17, 1934; Minutes, Ladies' Council Panther Boys' Club, Oct. 1934 [exact day not cited].

5. Copy of Ladies' Council of Panther Boys' Club, letter to Mr. Thomson, Dr. McLean and Board of Directors of Panther Boys' Club, Oct. 29, 1934, Hazel Vaughn Leigh Box, HVL Collection, FWPL. Miss Justice was enrolled at Texas Wesleyan College, where she would earn a degree in social work in 1939. Gibson interview.

6. Minutes, Board of Directors, Panther Boys' Club, Nov. 12, 1934, F. V. Thomson, secretary pro-tem, Minutes Box, HVL Collection, FWPL.

7. Minutes, PBC Women's Council, Nov. 26, 1934, Minutes Box, HVL Collection, FWPL.

8. Minutes of Committee Meeting of Committee appointed by Board of Directors of Panther Boys' Club, Dec. 6, 1934, Minutes Box, HVL Collection, FWPL. Also Resolution passed by Board of Directors of Panther Boys' Club, Dec. 10, 1934, ibid.

9. Mrs. Grover C. Leigh, letter to Board of Directors of Panther Boys' Club [1934], in Hazel Vaughn Leigh Box, HVL Collection, FWPL.

10. R. Robin McDonald, "Boys Clubs," *Fort Worth Star-Telegram,* no date, p. 12, in Clippings Box, HVL Collection, FWPL.

11. Dr. J. H. McLean, President of Panther Boys' Club Board of Directors, Dec. 14, 1934, to Mrs. Grover C. Leigh, President and members of the Woman's Council of PBC, in Hazel Vaughn Leigh Box, HVL Collection, FWPL.

12. Handwritten note by HVL on letter from Dr. McLean in Hazel Vaughn Leigh Box, HVL Collection, FWPL. Also "The History of the Beginning of Why the Fort Worth Boys' Club was organized by the Ladies," two handwritten pages in Hazel Vaughn Leigh Box, HVL Collection, FWPL.

13. Graham Ball interview. Also Michie Brous, interview by author, Fort Worth, Nov. 19, 1997.

14. Oral Interview, "Hazel Vaughn Leigh," p. 6.

15. Minutes, FWBC Ladies' Council, Jan. 10, 1935; Table in George D. Strayer, *Report of the Survey of the Schools of Fort Worth, Texas,* p. 94.

16. Oral Interview, "Hazel Vaughn Leigh," p. 7; Also Minutes, FWBC, Jan. 10, 1935.

17. Pate, *North of the River,* pp. 54–55; Dr. Delbert Derrett, interview by author, Fort Worth, Sept. 5, 1997. Objectives of Kiwanis in files of Derrett.

18. Paul Johnson, interview by author, Fort Worth, Dec. 4, 1997.

19. Muriel Gilder, interview by author, Fort Worth, Dec. 12, 1997.

20. Mary Crutcher, "Summer Sketchbook," *Fort Worth Press,* July 15, 1964, p. 4.; also ten page, typed "Early History of Fort Worth Boys' Club Council," in "Historical Notes" Folder in History Box 1, HVL Collection, FWPL. The address of the church was 1600 Boulevard.

21. "Early History of Fort Worth Boys' Club Council," p. 2.

22. "Fort Worth Boys' Club Opening Day February 1, 1935," five pages, mimeographed, HVL Collection, FWPL.

23. FWBC Minutes, Jan. 24, 1935, Minutes Box, HVL Collection, FWPL.

24. Pat Gordon, "Accident turned into life's work," *Fort Worth Metro,* Aug. 30, 1981, in Scrapbook, Hazel Vaughn Leigh 1935–1973, HVL Collection, FWPL.

25. Oral Interview, "Hazel Vaughn Leigh," p. 7.

26. Typewritten "History of the Fort Worth Boys' Club Council," two pages in "Historical Notes" Folder in History Box 1, HVL Collection, FWPL.

27. Gordon, "Accident turned into life's work."

28. FWBC, Inc., letter to Fort Worth Community Chest, Sept. 23, 1935, in Correspondence Box, HVL Collection, FWPL. Also Handwritten Note in "Historical Notes" Folder, History Box 1, Ibid.

29. Oral Interview, "Hazel Vaughn Leigh," p. 7.

30. Pat Patrick's Mar. 1, 1973, article in brown scrapbook #2, HVL Collection, FWPL. Also "Fort Worth Boys' Club Opening Day February 1, 1935," p. 5.

31. Crutcher, "Summer Sketchbook," p. 4.

CHAPTER 6

1. "Fort Worth Boys' Club Opening Day February 1, 1935," p. 5; Also "Church Gymnasium Becomes Haven For 205 Boys of Club," *Fort Worth Star-Telegram,* Sat., Feb. 2, 1935. Clipping in black scrapbook, 1935–37, HVL Collection, FWPL.

2. Some sources cite 135 boys, others 175. Two-page typewritten "History of the Fort Worth Boys' Club Council," p. 2, in "Historical Notes," Folder in History Box 1, HVL Collection, FWPL. Ten-page typed "Early History of Fort Worth Boys' Club Council," Ibid., p. 3; also Oral History, "Hazel Vaughn Leigh," p. 8; "Fort Worth Boys' Club Opening Day February 1, 1935," p. 5, Box (unidentified), HVL Collection, FWPL.

3. Minutes, FWBC Ladies' Council, Report for Year 1935, Jan. 19, 1936, Minutes Box, HVL Collection, FWPL; also Pat Patrick, Mar. 1, 1973, in black scrapbook, HVL Collection, FWPL.

4. Oral Interview, "Hazel Vaughn Leigh," p. 12.

5. Ten-page typed "Early History of Fort Worth Boys' Club Council," p. 3, in "Historical Notes" Folder in History Box 1, HVL Collection, FWPL.

6. Hall, *100 Years and Millions of Boys,* p. vii.

7. Oral Interview, "Hazel Vaughn Leigh," p. 12.

8. Minutes, Fort Worth Boys' Club, Feb. 11, 1935, HVL Collection, FWPL.

9. Oral Interview, "Hazel Vaughn Leigh," p. 19.

10. Ibid.

11. Minutes, Fort Worth Boys' Club, Apr. 8, 1935, HVL Collection, FWPL; also clipping, Apr. 29, 1935, in black scrapbook, HVL Collection, FWPL.

12. Minutes, May 13, 1935, HVL Collection, FWPL. FWBC Women's Council officers at this time were: Mrs. Grover C. Leigh, president; Mrs. Ed. Lowden, first vice president; Mrs. C. A. Lupton, second vice president; Mrs. Frank Fillingin, third vice president; Mrs. R. H. Kilpatrick, fourth vice president; Mrs. H. B. Simcox, secretary; and Mrs. Bert F. Weekley, corresponding secretary; Mrs. J. C. Maxwell, treasurer; Mrs. Ernest Allen, parliamentarian; Board Members were Mrs. Sam Vaughn, Mrs. A. L. Shuman, Mrs. J. L. Rawley, Mrs. Morgan Bryan, Mrs. T. H. Conner, and Mrs. A. L. Camp. Clipping in black scrapbook, 1935–1937, HVL Collection, FWPL.

13. Clipping in black scrapbook, 1935–1937, HVL Collection, FWPL. Also clipping, July 7, 1935, "Saturday Morning Program Added by Garden Center," Ibid. It was Charter Number 67765. Alberto R. Gonzales, Secretary of State, letter to author, Oct. 12, 1998.

14. Ten-page typed "Early History of Fort Worth Boys' Club Council," p. 6, in "Historical Notes" Folder in History Box 1, HVL Collection, FWPL.

15. Minutes, FWBC, Called Meeting, Sept. 18, 1935, Minutes Box, HVL Collection, FWPL.

16. Minutes, FWBC, Sept. 23, 1935, HVL Collection, FWPL.

17. Ibid., Oct. 14, 1935.

18. "World War Nurses to Honor Rogers," Nov. 21, 1935, clipping in black scrapbook, 1935–1937, in HVL Collection, FWPL.

19. Minutes, FWBC, Nov. 13, 1935, HVL Collection, FWPL; also "The Mission of the Fort Worth Boys' Club In The Community" (Radio Address) 1940, six pages typed text in "Historical Folder" in History Box 1, HVL Collection, FWPL. Otis Snow went to the radio station with her to help explain the club. She had the text written out for him; also ten pages typed "Early History of Fort Worth Boys' Club Council," p. 7, in Ibid.

20. "Mrs. Bryan Announces Committee," Fri., Nov. 22, 1935, clipping in black scrapbook, 1935–1937, HVL Collection, FWPL.

21. Minutes, FWBC, Specially called meeting, Nov. 18, 1935, and Minutes, FWBC, Dec. 10, 1935, HVL Collection, FWPL.

22. Clipping in black scrapbook, 1935–1937, HVL Collection, FWPL.

23. C. C. "Corky" Makarwich, interview by author, Fort Worth, Sept. 11, 1997; Bob Machos, interview by author, Fort Worth, Sept. 15, 1997; and Julian "Snooky" Pressley, telephone interview by author, July 17, 1997. Also Phipps, "Boys' Club Founder Recalls Rough Start," p. 25.

24. David A. Shannon, *Between the Wars: America, 1919–1941,* p. 163; also Makarwich interview; and Dixon Wecter, *The Age of the Great Depression 1929–1941,* p. 87.

25. Minutes, FWBC Council, Jan. 13, 1936. Dr. Greines had one sister who was a teacher. When New Testament scriptures were read in the classroom, she generally stepped out in the hall.

26. Minutes, FWBC Council, Jan. 13, 1936, HVL Collection, FWPL.

27. Gordon, "Accident turned into life's work."

28. Frank Perkins, "Kids From North Side Streets Now Leaders Here," *The News-Tribune,* Mar. 27, 1981, p. 3.

29. Machos interview.

30. Gordon, "Accident turned into life's work."

31. Handwritten History Notes, FWBC, in History Box 1, HVL Collection, FWPL.

32. Nov. 24, 1935, clipping in black scrapbook, 1935–1937; also 1935 Annual Report.

33. Ten-page typed "Early History of Fort Worth Boys' Club Council," in "Historical Notes" Folder in History Box 1, HVL Collection, FWPL.

34. Clipping in black scrapbook, 1935–1937.

35. Christopher Evans, "Personalities For the Boys," *Fort Worth Star-Telegram,* May 31, 1992, section E, p. 5.

36. Clipping in black scrapbook, 1935–1937; also Buddy Carter, interview by author, Fort Worth, Oct. 9, 1997.

CHAPTER 7

1. John B. Davis, Secretary of Texas Centennial Livestock and Frontier Days Exposition, letter to Mrs. Grover C. Leigh, Jan. 15, 1936, in Correspondence Box, HVL Collection, FWPL.

2. "200 Women To Serve on Show Board Named," Jan. 11, 1936, clipping, Clippings Box, HVL Collection, FWPL.

3. "Dedication Ceremonies at America's Playground," *The Fort Worth Press,* July 19, 1936, in Mary Daggett Lake Collection, Series XIII, Articles by Others, "Frontier Centennial," FWPL. Knight, *Fort Worth: Outpost on the Trinity,* p. 209.

4. Typed biography sheet on HVL in Correspondence Box 2, HVL Collection, FWPL.

5. Clipping in black scrapbook, 1935–1937, HVL Collection, FWPL.

6. Copy of a story by Julian Pressley, HVL Collection, FWPL.

7. Ten page "Early History of Fort Worth Boys' Club Council," pp. 7–8, in History Box 1; also Clipping in Box of Clippings, 1938–1975, HVL Collection, FWPL.

8. Minutes, FWBC, Mar. 9, 1936, and Minutes, FWBC, July 1, 1936, HVL Collection, FWPL.

9. Minutes, FWBC, July 1, 1936, Semi-Annual Report, HVL Collection, FWPL.

10. Minutes, FWBC, Sept. 14, 1936, HVL Collection, FWPL.

11. "F.W.B.C. Council," handwritten in "History Notes" FWBC Folder in History Box l; also Minutes, FWBC, Sept. 14, 1936, HVL Collection, FWPL.

12. Clipping in black scrapbook, 1935–1937, HVL Collection, FWPL.

13. Minutes, FWBC, Oct. 13, 1936; Minutes, Specially Called Meeting, Oct. 14, 1936; Minutes, FWBC, Oct. 19, 1936, in HVL Collection, FWPL.

14. Application for Corporation, Oct. 31, 1936, in Hazel Vaughn Leigh Box, HVL Collection, FWPL.

15. Pamphlet, "The Fort Worth Boys' Club," 1936, in Hazel Vaughn Leigh Box; also FWBC, Nov. 1936 Monthly Report, HVL Collection, FWPL.

16. Minutes, FWBC Council, Nov. 2, 1936; "Boys' Club Fund May Be Swelled By Visit Plan," Nov. 13, 1936, Clipping in black scrapbook, 1935–1937; Minutes, Specially Called Meeting, FWBC Council, Nov. 23, 1936, HVL Collection, FWPL.

17. "Panther Boys Have Birthday," Fort Worth Star-Telegram, Nov. 18, 1936, morning edition, Fort Worth Star-Telegram Clipping File, "Panther Boys' Club," UTA Special Collections.

18. "Panther Boys Report Issued," Fort Worth Star-Telegram, Sun., Jan. 24, 1937, Fort Worth Star-Telegram Clippings, UTA.

19. Clipping in black scrapbook, 1935–1937; Makarwich interview; also FWBC Council Monthly Report, Dec. 1936, HVL Collection, FWPL.

20. Makarwich interview.

21. Ibid.; Carter interview.

22. Machos interview.

23. Makarwich interview.

24. Ibid.

25. Picture and Cutline in Fort Worth Press, Mon., Mar. 30, 1936, in black scrapbook, 1935–1937; Copy of a story by Julian Pressley, HVL Collection, FWPL. Also Pressley interview.

26. Machos interview.

27. Typed Radio Address about Boys' Club in Radio Addresses Folder in History Box 2, HVL Collection, FWPL.

28. Photo, "Artist's Conception of Future Home of Fort Worth Boys' Club," *Fort Worth Star-Telegram,* Wed., Apr. 7, 1937, p. 9. Also 1937 Clipping on a page out of order in brown scrapbook 5, HVL Collection, FWPL.

29. "Work On Boys' Club Building to Begin In Few Weeks; Marks Great Progressive Movement," *North Fort Worth News,* Fri., Oct. 16, 1936, in black scrapbook, 1935–1937; also Minutes, FWBC, Inc., Nov. 21, 1936; and Minutes, FWBC, Inc., Nov. 30, 1936, HVL Collection, FWPL.

30. Ten typewritten pages, "Early History of the FWBC Council," p. 9.

31. Pressley interview; Clipping in black scrapbook, 1935–1937; also Minutes, FWBC, Inc., Apr. 13, 1937.

32. Fort Worth Boys' Club, Inc., Annual Report, Summary of History, 1972; Also Oral Interview, "Hazel Vaughn Leigh," p. 9.

33. Clipping in Scrapbook, 1937–1943, HVL Collection, FWPL; also Minutes, FWBC, Inc., July 7, 1937; also Minutes, FWBC, Inc., Aug. 25, 1937, in HVL Collection, FWPL.

34. "Members of Boys' Club Occupy New Quarters," Sept. 11, 1937, Clipping in scrapbook, 1937–1943, HVL Collection, FWPL.

35. Clipping in brown scrapbook 2; "200 Boys Swarm Into Play Home," undated clipping in Box of Clippings, HVL Collection, FWPL.

36. Cutlines under three photos to go with Edith Alderman Guedry Column, "From A Woman's Corner," *The Fort Worth Press,* Jan. 21, 1944, section 2, p. 1. Mrs. Hart's husband and his brother Martin owned all the property in the North Side along Main Street from Twenty-fifth Street to Twenty-eighth. They built a sturdy brick building where they planned to operate a meat packing facility to compete with Swift and Armour, but discontinued their plans. As of 1999 the building is the home of Los Vaqueros Mexican Restaurant. Also clippings in brown scrapbook, 1937–1943.

37. Clipping in black scrapbook, 1935–1937; "Public Welfare," *Fort Worth Press,* June 14, 1928, in Federal Writers' Project *Research Data,* Vol. 29, p. 21499; Also "History Notes on FWBC," in History Box 1, HVL Collection, FWPL. Minutes, FWBC, Inc., Nov. 23, 1937.

38. Clipping in black scrapbook, 1935–1937, HVL Collection, FWPL.

39. "Men's Show," Tues., Jan. 25, 1938, clipping in brown scrapbook, 1937–1943, HVL Collection, FWPL. Also "Fort Worth Boys' Club Council Favorite Recipes," published June 1938, was dedicated to Mrs. Grover Leigh, president of the council, in HVL Collection, FWPL.

40. Loose page, typed, 1938, in "Historical Notes" Folder in History Box 1, HVL Collection, FWPL. Also Letter, C. P. Little, Jr., National Youth Administration District Supervisor, to Mrs. Grover Leigh, Apr. 12, 1938, HVL Collection; and Pate, *Livestock Legacy,* p. 176.

41. 1939 Community Chest Flyer in Box of Clippings, HVL Collection, FWPL; also Minutes, FWBC, Inc., Aug. 20, 1938, HVL Collection, FWPL.

42. *Fort Worth City Directory,* 1938–39, p. 507, and 1940, p. 523.

CHAPTER 8

1. Actually only Hicks Field reopened; later a military base would be constructed on the west side of Fort Worth; it would be known as Carswell AFB for forty-five years.

2. From several clippings in brown scrapbook, 1937–1943; "North Side Boys' Club Work Grows," Jan. 11, 1939; Geren, Jr., interview; and Incorporation of Fort Worth Boys' Club Council, Jan. 24, 1939, Charter No. 74565, HVL Collection, FWPL.

3. Proposed Budget submitted to Community Chest for the budget year ending Nov. 30, 1939, "Hazel Vaughn Leigh" Box, HVL Collection, FWPL.

4. Atkinson, *The Boys' Club,* in "Boys' Club by R. K. Atkinson" Folder, HVL Collection, FWPL.

5. Clipping in brown scrapbook, 1960–1962 (stray page included); Jan. 21, 1939, clipping in brown scrapbook, 1937–1943, HVL Collection, FWPL.

6. Otis Snow, "Chest Assists City's Youth through Club," *Fort Worth Star-Telegram,* Nov. (day unclear), 1939, evening edition, *Fort Worth Star-Telegram* Clipping File, "Fort Worth Boys' Club," UTA Special Collections. Also clipping in brown scrapbook, 1960–1962 (page out of order), HVL Collection, FWPL.

7. "Fort Worth Boys' Club News," Vol. 1 No. 1, Wed., Mar. 20, 1940, one, legal-sized, mimeographed page in "Historical Notes" Folder in History Box 1, HVL Collection, FWPL.

8. "Fuller to Speak," Sat., July 22, 1939, clipping in brown scrapbook, HVL Collection, FWPL.

9. "Work Copy" of taped interview May 21, 1986, at Annual Meeting, cut to ten minutes, in "Historical Notes" Folder in History Box 1, HVL Collection, FWPL; also "Convention Report Boston, Mass.," 1940, Ibid.

10. Minutes, FWBC, Inc., May 7, 1941; also Dr. Abe Greines, letter to David Armstrong, Director, Boys' Clubs of America, Inc., June 13, 1941, HVL Collection, FWPL.

11. David W. Armstrong, Acting Executive Director, Boys' Clubs of America, Inc., letter to Dr. Abe Greines, June 24, 1941, in HVL Collection, FWPL.

12. Minutes, FWBC, Inc., Aug. 2, 1940, in HVL Collection, FWPL.

13. Six-page, typed radio speech, Aug. 28, 1940, in "Historical Notes" Folder in History Box 1, HVL Collection, FWPL. She had penciled in commas to indicate where to pause in reading the text.

14. Hazel Vaughn Leigh, letter to Dean Colby D. Hall, May 20, 1942; and S. W. Hutton, Registrar, letter to Hazel Vaughn Leigh, May 29, 1942, both in "Education TCU" Folder in History Box 1, HVL Collection, FWPL.

15. Oral Interview, "Hazel Vaughn Leigh," p. 12; and cutlines under three photos to go with Edith Alderman Guedry column, "From a Woman's Corner," *The Fort Worth Press,* Jan. 21, 1944, section 2, p. 1.

16. "Woman Founder of Boys' Club Will Get Degree at 46," *Fort Worth Star-Telegram,* May 21, 1944, *Fort Worth Star-Telegram* Clippings, "Hazel Vaughn Leigh," UTA Special Collections. Also "Women Finish TCU While Holding Full-Time Jobs," June 21, 1944, Ibid.

17. Texas Christian University Graduation Program, 1944; TCU Grade Report, "Education TCU" Folders 1943, 1944, in History Box 1, HVL Collection, FWPL. Also "Woman Founder of Boys' Club Will Get Degree at 46."

18. Machos interview. When Machos returned from the war, he went into the printing business. Mrs. Leigh often called on him for free printing for the club, and he always obliged.

19. Work Copy for Taping, Handwritten "Historical Notes" Folder in History Box 1, HVL Collection, FWPL.

20. Program of Annual Convention BCA, Inc., June 2–5, 1941, Hotel Commodore, New York, N.Y., in box labeled "Annual Reports BCA," HVL Collection, FWPL.

21. Text of Radio Interview on Community Chest Program, Jan. 22, 1941, p. 3.

22. "Panther Boys' Club Director Enlists for Pilot Training," *Fort Worth Star-Telegram,* Nov. 18, 1942, morning edition, *Fort Worth Star-Telegram* Clipping Collection, UTA Special Collections. Also Walter M. Hall, Director Program and Personnel Service, to Miss Martha Justice, Dec. 18, 1942, in Martha Justice Ball Collection, FWPL.

23. "Panther Boys Leaders Named," *Fort Worth Star-Telegram,* Feb. 11, 1942, morning edition, *Fort Worth Star-Telegram* Clippings, UTA Special Collections.

24. Walker, "Big Sister to the Panther Boys Says," p. 4; and Miss Martha Justice, typed notes of a speech she gave to Rotary Club during World War II, pp. 7–8, in Martha Justice Ball Collection, FWPL.

25. "Miss Martha Justice 'Grew Up' With Panther Boys' Club and Now She's 'Head Man'" *Fort Worth Star-Telegram,* Nov. 18, 1942, evening edition, *Fort Worth Star-Telegram* Clippings "Panther Boys' Club," UTA Special Collections. Also Cpl. Otis C. Snow, V-Mail to Mrs. Leigh and Boys, May 7, 1943, in History Box 2, HVL Collection, FWPL. Also Mary Sears, "Boys' Club Council Even Busier Than Usual With War Problems to Solve," *Fort Worth Star-Telegram,* Sun., Oct. 24, 1943, section 4, p. 4.

26. Work copy of interview taped May 21, 1986, at Annual Meeting, in "Historical Notes" Folder in History Box 1, p. 6, HVL Collection, FWPL.

27. Typed Radio Address about Boys' Club in "Radio Addresses" Folder in History Box 2, HVL Collection, FWPL.

28. Pate, *Livestock Legacy,* pp. 187–88.

29. Minutes, FWBC, Inc., Sept. 10, 1942; also Hazel Vaughn Leigh to Dr. Abe Greines, Sept. 11, 1942, Correspondence Box, HVL Collection, FWPL.

30. Copy of Income Tax Returns, 1941, 1942, 1943, in box labeled "Deeds and Leases" HVL Collection, FWPL.

31. Cards and items in "Grover Leigh" Folder in History Box 1, HVL Collection, FWPL.

32. "G. C. Leigh, 54, Injured, Dies," and "Train Costs Life of Grover Leigh," Clippings in "Grover Leigh" Folder in History Box 1, HVL Collection, FWPL.; also "Death of Leigh Accidental," *Fort Worth Star-Telegram,* Jan. 14, 1943, evening edition, p. 1.

33. Ruby Kerr, telephone interview by author, Feb. 23, 1998; also canceled check in "Grover Leigh" Folder in History Box 1, HVL Collection, FWPL.

34. Beverly Fogle, one of the nurses who stayed with Mrs. Leigh at Trinity Terrace, telephone interview by author, July 27, 1998.

35. Fred Baker Porter, "Indices of Social Organization and Disorganization in Fort Worth by Areas As Related To The Problems of Youth," MA Thesis, Texas Christian University, 1946, p. 47; and "Women Finish TCU While Holding Full-Time Jobs," *Fort Worth Star-Telegram,* May 21, 1944, *Fort Worth Star-Telegram* Clippings, "Hazel Vaughn Leigh," UTA Special Collections; also "500 Boys Will Attend Party," *Fort Worth Star-Telegram,* Dec. 21, 1944, evening edition, *Fort Worth Star-Telegram* Clippings, UTA Special Collections.

36. Minutes, FWBC, Inc., Nov. 24, 1944, and Minutes, FWBC Council, Jan. 17, 1945, HVL Collection, FWPL.

37. "Soldier to Lead Allegiance Pledge of Boys' Club," undated clipping in Clippings Box, 1940–1969, HVL Collection, FWPL.

38. "The Fort Worth Boys' Club News" [mimeographed] 1945 in "History Notes" Folder in History Box 1, HVL Collection, FWPL; also "Three

More Members of Boys' Club To Enter Service; They Join Over 500," *Fort Worth Star-Telegram,* July 12, 1945, in Clippings Box, 1940–1969, HVL Collection, FWPL; also Bill Burklow, telephone interview by author, Aug. 17, 1998.

39. Makarwich interview; Two-page typed article in "Historical Notes" in History Box 1, HVL Collection, FWPL; and "Copy of a story by Julian Pressley," typewritten in HVL Collection, FWPL.

40. "Waste Fat Drive Will Go Ahead Thru Boys' Club," *North Fort Worth News,* Apr. 28, 1944, p. 1.

41. Oral Interview, "Hazel Vaughn Leigh," p. 21.

42. Virginia (Gee Gee) King, interview by author, Fort Worth, Feb. 20, 1998.

43. "To Re-establish Headquarters Rotarians Will Be Urged to Sponsor Panther Boys' Club Fund Campaign," *Fort Worth Star-Telegram,* May 27, 1947, morning edition, *Fort Worth Star-Telegram* Clipping File, "Panther Boys' Club," UTA Special Collections. Eventually the Amon Carter Foundation and Perry Bass bought the Central Methodist Church adjacent to the Lipscomb property and doubled the PBC size. Mack Williams, "In Old Fort Worth: L. B. Price Gave His Life to Start Panther Boys' Club," *Fort Worth News-Tribune,* Dec. 19, 1986, p. 8B. Also "Trinity Church Bought For Home of Boys' Club," *Fort Worth Star-Telegram,* Jan. 25, 1948, morning edition, *Fort Worth Star-Telegram* Clipping File, UTA Special Collections.

44. "Plans Set for Boys' Club Site," *Fort Worth Star-Telegram,* Jan. 24, 1947, *Fort Worth Star-Telegram* Clipping File "Panther Boys' Club," UTA Special Collections. Also Graham Ball interview.

45. "Loss Conceded Cupid Wins Bout With Boys' Club," *Fort Worth Star-Telegram,* June 15, 1947, *Fort Worth Star-Telegram* Clipping File, "Panther Boys' Club" UTA Special Collections; also "Member Organizations of the Boys' Clubs of America, Inc.," p. iii (1946) in Martha Justice Ball Collection, FWPL; and William Edwin Hall, President BCA, Inc., letter to Mrs. Graham Ball, July 1, 1947, Ibid.; *The Communicator,* Fort Worth Community Chest, July 1946. Photo and Cutline, p. 5, in Ibid.

46. "Loss Conceded Cupid Wins Bout With Boys' Club"; "Panther Boys' Club to Have New Director," *Fort Worth Star-Telegram,* July 11, 1947, in *Fort Worth Star-Telegram* Clipping File, "Panther Boys' Club," UTA Special Collections.

47. Martha Justice Ball to Gordon Grines, Oct. 22, 1947, in Martha Justice Ball Collection, FWPL.

48. Graham Ball interview. Mrs. Martha Justice Ball died in 1981. Her husband, in his eighties, admitted that newspaper articles, including his wife's obituary, were wrong about Martha's being the first woman executive director of a boys' club. Hazel preceded her. He said there was one other

woman executive director of a boys' club in New England and that two
sisters had started the very first boys' club in Philadelphia in the 1860s.
When asked if Hazel and Martha were friendly at national Boys' Clubs of
America, Inc., conventions through the years, which they all attended, he
said, "No." Hazel snubbed Martha but spoke to him. Martha had explained
to him that Hazel's break with the PBC in 1934 had been over a disagreement with the executive director, F. V. Thomson. If she knew that Hazel
and the ladies were mad at her for several reasons, including her inatten-
tiveness in letting the materials they donated slip away and be sold, she
apparently did not indicate it to her husband.

49. "Panther Boys' Club to Have New Director"; "New Panther Club Director
Takes Office," *Fort Worth Star-Telegram,* July 22, 1947, p. 10.

50. Clipping in Clippings Box, HVL Collection, FWPL; also Vaughn Family
Clippings in History Box 2, Ibid.

51. Two-page typed untitled news article, Aug. 7, 1947, in "Historical Notes"
folder in History Box 1, HVL Collection, FWPL; also Irvin Farman,
Tandy's Money Machine.

52. "National Boys' Club Week To Be Observed by Panthers," *Fort Worth Star-
Telegram,* Mar. 27, 1949, morning edition, *Fort Worth Star-Telegram* Clipping
File, "Panther Boys' Club," UTA Special Collections.

53. Pate, *North of the River,* pp. 141–42; Oral Interview, "Hazel Vaughn Leigh,"
p. 15; and Minutes, FWBC Council, Nov. 28, 1949, HVL Collection,
FWPL.

54. "H. S. Vaughn TCU Athletic Great, Is Dead," *Fort Worth Star-Telegram,* July
5, 1949, morning edition, pp. 1–2.

55. Eileen Snyder, interview by author, Fort Worth, Feb. 6, 1998.

CHAPTER 9

1. Amon G. Carter, Sr., to Mr. J. A. "Tiny" Gooch, Dec. 29, 1950,
Correspondence Box 2, HVL Collection, FWPL; also Kris Drummond,
interview by author, Fort Worth, Nov. 12, 1997.

2. Edith Deen, "From A Woman's Corner: Mrs. Leigh Loves Work With
Boys," *The Fort Worth Press,* Thurs., May 29, 1952, p. 22; also Clyde E.
Comer, Partner Home Investment Company, to Hazel Vaughn Leigh, Dec.
29, 1958, in Deeds and Leases Box, HVL Collection, FWPL.

3. "350 Youngsters Celebrate Boys' Club's 16th Birthday," *Fort Worth Star-
Telegram,* Feb. 14, 1951, morning edition, Clippings Box, 1940–1969,
HVL Collection, FWPL; also "Boys' Club to Hold 16th Birthday Party,"
North Fort Worth News, Fri., Feb. 9, 1951.

4. Barbara Moore, "Courageous Woman Loves Boy Clubbers," *Fort Worth Star-Telegram,* Oct. 8, 1956, p. 8; and "Olympic Star Got His Start Worries of Many Working Mothers Solved by Fort Worth Boys' Club," *Fort Worth Star-Telegram,* Sept. 12, 1952, morning edition, *Fort Worth Star-Telegram* Clipping File, UTA Special Collections.

5. Clipping in Clippings Box, 1938–1975, HVL Collection, FWPL.

6. Edith Deen, "From a Woman's Corner, Mrs. Leigh Loves Work With Boys," *The Fort Worth Press,* May 29, 1952, p. 22.

7. King interview; and "He's The Champ: Lad Proud Of Freckles Has Reason," *Fort Worth Star-Telegram,* June 27, 1953, morning edition, *Fort Worth Star-Telegram* Clippings, UTA Special Collections, Arlington.

8. Deen, "From a Woman's Corner," p. 22.

9. Funeral Book for Samuel Vaughn in History Box 2, HVL Collection, FWPL; also Sam Vaughn Clippings Folder in Ibid.

10. Sam Vaughn, letter to Hazel, Jan. 25, 1953, in Deeds and Leases Box, HVL Collection, FWPL.

11. "History of the Boys' Club Movement," one page typed in "Historical Notes" Folder in History Box 1, HVL Collection, FWPL.

12. Brous interview; also "Boys' Club News," by HVL, undated clipping in Clippings Box, 1938–1975; also same article in *North Fort Worth News,* Feb. 8, 1957.

13. "Mrs. Leigh to Attend 51st Nat'l Boys' Club Convention," *The News,* Thurs., May 9, 1957, p. 8.

14. Hazel Leigh, "Local Club Takes Part In National Boys' Club Week," *North Fort Worth News,* Apr. 4, 1957, p. 1.

15. Ibid.

16. Scrapbook No. 10, Pictures of Conferences, University of New York, Roster, 1958; Photo of Arch in New York City and comments, Photo Box 4, HVL Collection, FWPL.

17. "J. A. Gooch Given Award For Long Boys' Club Service," *Fort Worth Star-Telegram,* Apr. 11, 1959, p. 22.

18. "Governor Names Boys' Club Head To Youth Panel," *Fort Worth Star-Telegram,* Jan. 30, 1959, morning edition, *Fort Worth Star-Telegram* Clippings, UTA.

19. Lyndon B. Johnson to Mrs. Hazel Vaughn Leigh, Jan. 19, 1960, and Jim Wright to Mrs. Hazel Vaughn Leigh, Feb. 10, 1960, both in scrapbook "Hazel Vaughn Leigh," 1935–1973, HVL Collection, FWPL.

20. Catherine Gunn, "Boys' Club Director To Receive National Award," no date, in Scrapbook No. 3, 1961–1962, HVL Collection, FWPL; also May 3, 1960, clipping in brown scrapbook No. 5, HVL Collection, FWPL.

21. Drummond and King interviews.

22. "Hold On There, Pardner," cutline under photo in *Fort Worth Star-Telegram,* Feb. 5, 1960, morning edition, in Clippings Box, 1940–1969, HVL Collection, FWPL.

23. Minutes, FWBC Council, Nov. 29, 1961; Cutline to Photo in Scrapbook No. 3, 1961–1962, HVL Collection, FWPL; also Clipping in *Fort Worth Press,* Dec. 8, 1961, in Ibid; and "Sale of Antiques Friday Will Aid Boys' Club Pool," *The Fort Worth Press,* June 6, 1962, p. 14.

24. Kent Biffle, "Hazel Leigh—She's the Mother for 3710 Boys at Club Here," *Fort Worth Press,* no date, clipping in brown scrapbook, 1960–1962, HVL Collection, FWPL; Minutes, FWBC Council, Jan. 31, 1962

25. "Earth Turned For New Pool At Boys' Club," *Fort Worth Star-Telegram,* Dec. 11, 1961, in Scrapbook No. 3, HVL Collection, FWPL; "Boys' Club Dedicates New Swimming Pool," *Fort Worth Star-Telegram,* July 21, 1962, in Clippings Box, 1940–1969, HVL Collection, FWPL.

26. Loose brochure in brown scrapbook, 1960–1962; Brous and Drummond interviews.

27. "Boys' Club Director To Serve Nationally," *Fort Worth Star-Telegram,* Fri., Mar. 20, 1964, no page cited, Clipping in Clippings Box, HVL Collection, FWPL.

28. Invitation to Texas Welcome Dinner for JFK in Austin Nov. 22, 1963, HVL Collection, FWPL.

29. Typed list of FWBC Council Expenditures 1935 to 1964 in Box labeled "Hazel Vaughn Leigh," HVL Collection, FWPL.

30. Minutes, FWBC Council, Oct. 7, and Nov. 18, 1963; also Certificate of Incorporation, Fort Worth Boys' Club Endowment Fund, Inc., Charter No. 199502, Jan. 13, 1964. Purposes: "To perpetuate and to assist in the defraying of the expenses of the Fort Worth Boys' Club, Inc., a benevolent, charitable and educational undertaking which assists and carries on the work of conserving the boy-life of Fort Worth by providing opportunities for the intellectual, spiritual, physical and social development of the boys of such community."

31. Paul Johnson interview; Minutes, FWBC, Inc., May 28, 1964; Minutes, FWBC, Inc., Feb. 20, 1964, HVL Collection, FWPL.

32. Photo with Christmas Card of House, Photo of Vaughn House, Photo Box 3, HVL Collection, FWPL; also Race, *Pioneer Fort Worth,* p. 101; also Nina Maria Cole, "Nina Maria's Notebook," *Fort Worth Press,* Mon., Apr. 7, 1969, p. 20.

33. Dr. Aubrey Sharpe, telephone interview by author, Sept. 22, 1997.

34. James E. Sperring, Regional Director of Boys' Clubs of America, Inc., to Mrs. Hazel Leigh, Aug. 11, 1967, in Scrapbook, Hazel Vaughn Leigh, 1935–1973, in HVL Collection, FWPL.

35. Mrs. Edwin H. Hughes, III, Women's Auxiliary Boys' Club Association of Indianapolis, Indiana, "The Women's Auxiliary and Communications," *The Journal Boys' Clubs of America* 3:4 (fall 1968): 39.

36. Treasurer's Report, FWBC Council, Dec. 1965.

37. Brous interview.

38. Brous interview; Minutes, FWBC, Inc., Apr. 7, 1965; and Joyce Chambers Kingston (relative of Hazel), letter to author, Sept. 24, 1997.

39. Minutes, FWBC, Inc., Aug. 11 and Nov. 21, 1966; also Minutes, FWBC Endowment Fund, Inc., Mar. 31, 1966, in Minutes Box, HVL Collection, FWPL.

40. Minutes, FWBC Council, Apr. 7, 1969, HVL Collection, FWPL.

Chapter 10

1. Drummond interview; Minutes, FWBC, Inc., Feb. 17, 1970; Minutes, FWBC Endowment Fund, Inc., Mar. 17, 1970; Minutes, FWBC, Inc., Mar. 17, 1970, HVL Collection, FWPL.

2. Minutes, FWBC, Inc., Apr. 29, 1970, HVL Collection, FWPL.

3. Minutes, FWBC, Inc., May 20, 1970, and Minutes, FWBC, Inc., July 22, 1970, HVL Collection, FWPL.

4. "History Notes" FWBC Folder in History Box 1; also Minutes, FWBC, Inc., Sept. 9, 1971, HVL Collection, FWPL.

5. "Greatest need is boys' camp," *The Press,* Feb. 5, 1971, p. 15.

6. Minutes, FWBC Endowment Fund, Inc., Apr. 4, 1972, HVL Collection, FWPL.

7. Fort Worth Boys' Club Annual Report, 1972, HVL Collection, FWPL.

8. "Founder Retires: Boys' Club Honors Mrs. Hazel Leigh," undated clipping in black scrapbook, HVL Collection, FWPL.

9. Telegrams and letters in scrapbook, Hazel Vaughn Leigh, 1935–1973; Thomas Craighead to Hazel Vaughn Leigh, May 29, 1973, in Ibid.; William R. Bricker, National Director Boys' Clubs of America, to Hazel Vaughn Leigh, Apr. 26, 1973, all in HVL Collection, FWPL.

10. Clare Eyrich, "Hazel Leigh: Boys 'Best Friend,'" clipping in black scrapbook; and Lloyd Stewart, column, 1973, in brown scrapbook No. 2, Clippings 1970–1975, HVL Collection, FWPL.

11. Handwritten copy of remarks made by Margaret Owens, May 17, 1973, at Ridglea Country Club Luncheon hosted by the Fort Worth Boys' Club Council and Board, HVL Collection, FWPL.

12. Howard G. Wible, President, Fort Worth Public Library Board, letter to Mrs. Hazel Leigh, May 29, 1973; Jack W. Green, City Secretary, letter to Mrs. Hazel Leigh, Aug. 2, 1977; and Minutes, FWBC, Inc., Dec. 15, 1975, in Scrapbook, Hazel Vaughn Leigh 1935–1973, HVL Collection, FWPL; also Invitation to Inaugural Festivities honoring Governor Dolph Briscoe, Jan. 21, 1975, in HVL Collection, FWPL.

13. Mona Sylvester, telephone interview by author, Jan. 26, 1998; also "Mrs. Leigh Heads New '93 Club Slate," Fort Worth Star-Telegram, May 2, 1975, p. 4B.

14. Gregor interview.

15. Minutes, FWBC, Inc., June 16, 1975; also "Boys' Club planning to start hall of fame," in brown scrapbook No. 5, 1960s, 1970s in HVL Collection, FWPL.

16. By-Laws of the Alumni Members of Fort Worth Boys' Club, Inc., in "Hazel Vaughn Leigh" Box, HVL Collection, FWPL; Minutes of first meeting of FWBC Alumni Association, Feb. 24, 1976, in Ibid.; Harry Heinecke, "Boys' Club, 42 Years Old, More Spry Than Ever," The News-Tribune, Apr. 1, 1977, p. 12; also Oral Interview, "Hazel Vaughn Leigh," p. 11.

17. Gregor interview; Barbara Wheeler, interview by author, Fort Worth, Oct. 6, 1997; and Minutes, FWBC, Inc., Oct. 20, 1975, in HVL Collection, FWPL.

18. James E. Sperring, Regional Director, BCA, Inc., letter to Hazel Leigh, July 12, 1974, Correspondence Box, HVL Collection, FWPL.

19. Minutes, FWBC Council, June 29, 1976; January 22, 1976, and June 21, 1977, Minutes Box, in HVL Collection, FWPL.

20. Minutes, FWBC, Inc., Sept. 15, 1970; Aug. 3 and Nov. 16, 1971, in HVL Collection, FWPL.

21. Minutes, FWBC, Inc., Oct. 1973, in HVL Collection, FWPL.

22. Minutes, FWBC, Inc., Nov. 19, 1973, HVL Collection, FWPL.

23. William R. Sarsgard, Chairman, Special Committee United Way of Metropolitan Tarrant County, letter to Mrs. Hazel Leigh, July 28, 1975, Correspondence Box 2, HVL Collection, FWPL.

24. Ibid.

25. Minutes, FWBC, Inc., July 19 and Sept. 20, 1976; Jan. 17, May 16, June 20 and Dec. 19, 1977, HVL Collection, FWPL.

26. William Sarsgard, former United Way Allocations Committee Chairman, telephone interview by author, July 29, 1998.

27. Minutes, FWBC Council, Sept. 24, 1975, HVL Collection, FWPL.

28. Minutes, FWBC, Inc., June 12, 1978, and handwritten notes on same; also Roger Lohn, Chairman Allocation Subcommittee IV, United Way of Metropolitan Tarrant County, letter to Mr. Gene Graves, President, FWBC, Inc., May 15, 1978, in Correspondence Box, HVL Collection, FWPL; also Minutes, FWBC, Inc., Apr. 19, 1976; Thomas L. Daniels, Regional Service Director, Boys' Clubs of America, letter to Mr. Gene Graves, May 31, 1978, in Correspondence Box, HVL Collection, FWPL; Annual Corporate Luncheon Minutes, FWBC, Inc., Apr. 24, 1979.

29. Minutes, FWBC, Inc., Jan. 7 and 21, 1974; also Letter from PB who resigned to DC, executive director, explaining why he resigned, with copy to Hazel Vaughn Leigh and Paul Johnson, current president of FWBC, Inc., Board, in Correspondence Box, HVL Collection, FWPL.

30. Roger Lohn, Chairman Allocation Committee, United Way of Metropolitan Tarrant County to Gene Graves, Jr., President, FWBC, Aug. 7, 1978, Correspondence Box, HVL Collection, FWPL.

31. Minutes, FWBC, Inc., Sept. 16, 1981; and Minutes, FWBC, Inc., July 16, 1980.

32. Agency Evaluation Committee Task Force: A Report on the Fort Worth Boys' Club by Planning and Research Council of United Way, Dec. 1978, pp. 2–3 in HVL Collection, FWPL.

33. Gene Graves, President, to Tommy Daniels, Regional Service Director, BCA, Inc., Dallas, June 1978, Correspondence Box 2, HVL Collection, FWPL.

34. Preston Bunnell, letter of resignation as Executive Director, to Gene Graves, President, FWBC, Inc., Jan. 1, 1978, in Correspondence Box 2, HVL Collection, FWPL.

35. Obituary, *Fort Worth Star-Telegram,* Nov. 24, 1978, in Box of Clippings, HVL Collection, FWPL.

36. Gene Graves, President, FWBC, Inc., letter to Mr. Roger Lohn, United Way, Mar. 12, 1979.

37. Agenda, First Annual Meeting Lone Star Area Council, BCA, Inc., in BCA Box, HVL Collection, FWPL; also Richard L. Honsaker, Executive Director, letter to Miss Barbara Birkhead, Chairman of Hercules Award, AAUW, Mar. 13, 1979, Correspondence Box 2, HVL Collection, FWPL.

38. James E. Sperring, Regional Director, BCA, Inc., letter to HVL, June 5, 1979.

39. Minutes, FWBC, Inc., Apr. 3, 1967, and Minutes, FWBC Endowment Fund, Inc., Feb. 9, 1967.

40. Brous interview; and Ann Petruccelli, United Way, telephone interview by author, July 28, 1998.

41. "History Notes, FWBC," FWBC Endowment Fund, Inc., Statement of Assets, Liability and Fund Balances, Dec. 15, 1974, HVL Collection, FWPL.

42. "FW Boys' Club Council First Meeting Monday," *Fort Worth Star-Telegram*, Sept. 23, 1970, Clipping in Scrapbook No. 2, 1970–1975, HVL Collection, FWPL; also Committee meeting notes, Aug. 16, 1975, Eagle Mountain Unit Box, Ibid.; Alvin Botts (Rattikin Title Company), letter to FWBC Endowment Fund, Inc., Oct. 6, 1975; also Minutes, FWBC Endowment Fund, Inc., Aug. 15, 1975; and "Report of Camp Committee to FWBC, Inc., Board," July 1975, Minutes Box, 1974–1988, HVL Collection, FWPL.

43. Minutes, FWBC Endowment Fund, Inc., Aug. 15, 1975; Oct. 24, 1975; and Minutes FWBC, Inc., Jan. 19, 1976.

44. Minutes, FWBC Endowment Fund, Inc., Mar. 26, 1976.

45. "Boys' club Unit attains ranch goal," *Fort Worth Star-Telegram*, May 7, 1979, in scrapbook, 1979–1980, HVL Collection, FWPL; Also Geren, Jr., interview.

46. Snyder interview; and Gloria Hawkins, telephone interview by author, Aug. 20, 1998. Her former husband, Reece Davis, owned Westgate Fabrics.

47. Minutes FWBC Council, Nov. 2, 1978.

48. "Agreement Between Fort Worth Boys' Club (Fort Worth Boys' Club Endowment Fund) and Less [sic] Peden and wife, Dixie Peden, 1979."

49. Snyder interview.

50. Scrapbook, 1979–1980, HVL Collection, FWPL.

51. Eagle Mountain Unit of the FWBC 1982 Objective Record Sheet in Eagle Mountain Unit Box, HVL Collection, FWPL; also "Planning & Research Council A Division of United Way of Metropolitan Tarrant County Staff Report," five pages in "Historical Notes" Folder in History Box 1, HVL Collection, FWPL.

52. "Planning & Research Council A Division of United Way of Metropolitan Tarrant County Staff Report," p. 4.

53. Program of Eagle Mountain Unit Dedication, Scrapbook, 1979–1980, HVL Collection, FWPL.

54. "Boys' Club unit dedicated locally," *Azle News,* May 24, 1979, in Scrapbook, 1979–1980; Minutes, FWBC Council, Aug. 21, 1978; "Boys'

Club unit attain ranch goal," *Fort Worth Star-Telegram,* May 7, 1978, in Scrapbook, 1979–1980, in HVL Collection, FWPL.

55. Gregor interview.

56. Roger Lohn, Chairman Allocation Sub Committee VI, United Way of Metropolitan Tarrant County, letter to Gene Graves, Jr., President, FWBC, Inc., Nov. 26, 1979.

57. Minutes, FWBC, Inc., Mar. 21, 1980.

58. "Auxiliary Helps Support Boys' Club," *Azle News Advertiser,* Feb. 14, 1980, section 2, p. 2.

59. "Boys' Club seeks 'fighting chance,'" *Azle News,* July 31, 1980, section 2, p. 5.

60. Tim Carpenter, interview by author, Azle, Texas, Aug. 7, 1997.

61. Carpenter interview; The boards voted in September 1994 to close at the end of 1994. Bob Buckel, "AISD to buy Boys' Club property," *The Azle News,* Aug. 17, 1995, pp. 1–2.

62. Carpenter interview.

63. Gerald Shinn, interview by author, Azle, Tex., July 29, 1997,; also Dr. Santo Forte, superintendent of Azle ISD, interview by author, Azle, Texas, July 31, 1997; also Buckel, "AISD to buy Boys' Club property"; Date of purchase by AISD was Aug. 15, 1995; price, $256,274; Minutes of the Board of Trustees of Azle Independent School District Regular Board Meeting, Aug. 15, 1995, four pages.

64. Paul Koeppe, interview by author, Fort Worth, Sept. 24, 1997.

CHAPTER 11

1. Koeppe interview; and Hazel Leigh, letter to Ron Gilley, Aug. 29, 1984, copy in HVL Collection, FWPL.

2. Koeppe interview.

3. Goodger interview; Lesbia Roberts, telephone interview by author, Oct. 24, 1997; and Snyder interview.

4. Koeppe and Brous interviews.

5. Minutes, FWBC, Inc., July 28, 1982, HVL Collection, FWPL.

6. Letter from FWBC Council, Inc., to Mr. J. A. (Tiny) Gooch, June 8, 1983, Articles of Incorporation Box, HVL Collection, FWPL; J. A. Gooch, letter to Board of Directors of FWBC Council, Oct. 1, 1984, Correspondence Box, HVL Collection, FWPL.

7. Minutes, FWBC, Inc., Nominating Committee Meeting, Sept. 29, 1983, HVL Collection, FWPL.

8. William R. Hinckley, letter to Hazel Vaughn Leigh, Nov. 15, 1983, in Hazel Vaughn Leigh Box, HVL Collection, FWPL; also Minutes, FWBC, Inc., Oct. 19, 1983; and Raymond Wilson, President, FWBC, Inc., letter to Mrs. Robert Craig, Secretary, FWBC Council, Oct. 20, 1983, HVL Collection, FWPL.

9. Mrs. Albert Gregor, President, FWBC Council, letter to Paul Koeppe, Treasurer, FWBC, Inc., Nov. 2, 1983, Lawsuit Box, HVL Collection, FWPL.

10. Koeppe interview.

11. J. O. "Trey" Shannon, III, interview by author, Fort Worth, Sept. 17, 1997.

12. Koeppe interview.

13. Shannon interview.

14. Goodger and Shannon interviews.

15. Shannon, Koeppe, and Johnson interviews.

16. Koeppe interview.

17. King interview.

18. Minutes, FWBC, Inc., Board of Directors Meeting, Nov. 22, 1983, HVL Collection, FWPL.

19. Snyder interview.

20. Executive Director's Report to FWBC, Inc., Board, Nov. 23, 1983; David Jackson, letter of resignation, Oct. 19, 1983, Minutes Box, 1974–1988, HVL Collection, FWPL.

21. Executive Director's Report to FWBC, Inc., Board, Nov. 23, 1983, in Minutes, 1974–1988 Box, HVL Collection, FWPL.

22. Gregor interview; and Mary Smith, interview by author, Fort Worth, Oct. 3, 1997.

23. Nelda Gregor, letter to Raymond Wilson, Dec. 6, 1983, in Lawsuit Box, HVL Collection, FWPL.

24. King interview.

25. Jim Stratton, former Regional Director, BCA, Inc., telephone interview by author, July 27, 1998. In 1998 Stratton was with the Scottsdale, Arizona, Boys' and Girls' Clubs.

26. Paul Koeppe, Treasurer, FWBC, Inc., Board, letter to Miller Goodger, President, FWBC Endowment Fund, Inc., Jan. 24, 1984, Minutes Box, HVL Collection, FWPL; Paul Koeppe, letter to Elaine Brown, President, FWBC Council, Jan. 25, 1984, Correspondence Box 2, HVL Collection, FWPL.

27. Minutes, FWBC Council, June 29, 1984; and Minutes, FWBC Endowment Fund, Inc., July 11, 1984, Minutes Box, HVL Collection, FWPL.

28. Minutes, FWBC, Inc., July 18, 1984.

29. Minutes, FWBC Endowment Fund, Inc., Dec. 12, 1984; Minutes, FWBC Council, Executive Board, Dec. 10, 1984; and Handwritten Notes in "History Notes," FWBC Folder in History Box 1, HVL Collection, FWPL.

30. Hazel's notes of Executive Committee Meeting, Dec. 23, 1984 in "Historical Notes" Folder in History Box 1, HVL Collection, FWPL; also Snyder interview.

31. Copy of Restraining Order in Lawsuit Box, HVL Collection, FWPL; also Miller Goodger, letter to FWBC Endowment Fund, Inc., Board Members, Jan. 4, 1985; and FWBC, Inc., vs. FWBC Endowment Fund, Inc., 153rd District Court 153-87536.

32. Michael Handy, Attorney for FWBC, Inc., letter to Miller Goodger, President, FWBC Endowment Fund, Inc., Feb. 20, 1985, in Minutes Box, HVL Collection, FWPL.

33. Gregor interview; Karen Schoenbucher, Chairman, Pro-tem, Allocations Subcommittee VI, United Way, letter to Mr. Tray [sic] Shannon, Aug. 15, 1984, in Correspondence Box 2, HVL Collection, FWPL; also "History Notes" FWBC Folder in History Box 1, Ibid.; also Minutes, FWBC Endowment Fund, Inc., July 31, 1985, p. 2.

34. Hawkins interview.

35. Brous and Graham Ball interviews.

36. Brous interview.

37. Minutes, FWBC Council, Inc., July 14, 1985.

38. Order of Dismissal, Apr. 18, 1986, No. 153-87536-85, Judge Sidney Farrar, Jr., dismissed the case because parties had agreed in Apr. 2, 1986, settlement, in Lawsuit Box, HVL Collection, FWPL.

39. Bill Hinckley to Hazel Vaughn Leigh, Aug. 29, 1986; and William R. Hinckley, Executive Director Boys' Clubs of Omaha, to Hazel Leigh, Oct. 27, 1986, Correspondence Box 2, HVL Collection, FWPL.

40. Bill Burklow, letter to Hazel Vaughn Leigh, July 28, 1986, Correspondence, HVL Collection, FWPL.

41. Mack Williams, "In Old Fort Worth: The Club That Built Men," Fort Worth News-Tribune, May 16, 1986, p. 19A.

42. Handwritten by HVL, Nov. 26, 1986, four days after the conversation. Also related in Minutes, FWBC Council, Inc., Feb. 26, 1987.

43. Ibid.

44. Shannon and Koeppe interviews.

45. Carter interview; Minutes, FWBC Endowment Fund, Inc., Mar. 3, 1988.

46. Michael Handy, letter to Fort Worth Boys' Club Endowment Fund, Inc., Mar. 16, 1988, in Lawsuit Box, HVL Collection, FWPL.

47. Plaintiff's Original Petition and Application for Temporary Restraining Order Cause No. 348-118749-89, Feb. 13, 1989, Lawsuit Box, HVL Collection, FWPL.

48. Ibid., Feb. 13, 1989, p. 7.

49. Handy, letter to Fort Worth Boys' Club Endowment Fund, Inc., Mar. 16, 1988; Handwritten undated notes, HVL; Mr. and Mrs. James L. West, letter to FWBC Endowment Fund, Inc., Oct. 29, 1980, Correspondence Box, HVL Collection, FWPL; also Richard L. Schleier, Jr., Attorney, letter to Walter L. O'Neill, FWBC Endowment Fund, Inc., Sept. 6, 1988, in Lawsuit Box, HVL Collection, FWPL.

50. Stratton interview; also Joe Cordova, executive director Boys' and Girls' Clubs of Greater Fort Worth, interview by author, Fort Worth, Sept. 29, 1997.

51. Jim Caufield, senior vice president of administrative services, Boys' and Girls' Clubs of America, Inc., telephone interview by author, Aug. 17, 1998.

52. "Panther and Fort Worth Boys' Clubs To Merge," *The Eagle Extra,* Dec. 1, 1989, p. 6; also Minutes, Boys' Club Merger Committee Meeting, Nov. 16, 1988, in Hazel Vaughn Leigh Box, HVL Collection, FWPL.

53. Plaintiff's Original Petition and Application for Temporary Restraining Order Cause No. 348-118749-89, Feb. 13, 1989; and Minutes, FWBC Council, Executive Committee Meeting, Sept. 29, 1988.

54. Plaintiff's Original Petition and Application for Temporary Restraining Order Cause No. 348-118749, Feb. 13, 1989, p. 10, in Lawsuit Box, HVL Collection, FWPL.

55. Ibid., pp. 10, 11, 13; also Shannon interview.

56. Michelle Marti, telephone interview by author, Sept. 20, 1997.

57. Gregor interview.

58. "Statement of Facts Temporary Injunction Hearing," Volume I, No. 348-118749-89, Fort Worth Boys' Club, Inc., vs. Boys' Club Endowment Fund, Inc., et al., Feb. 27, 1989, p. 212. Paul Koeppe, testimony at 1989 hearing, pp. 211–12, in Lawsuit Box, HVL Collection, FWPL.

59. 1989 Hearing, pp. 212–13.

60. Cause No. 348-118749-89 Order from Judge Michael D. Schattman to begin discussions, Feb. 28, 1989; and Michelle S. Marti, letter to Hazel Vaughn Leigh, Mrs. R. E. Snyder, Miss Rosemary Oliver, July 12, 1989, in Lawsuit Box, HVL Collection, FWPL.

61. "Statement of Position of the Fort Worth Boys' Club, Inc.," by their attorney, Michael Handy, pp. 6–8, in Lawsuit Box, HVL Collection, FWPL.

62. Stefani Gammage, "Boys clubs moving closer to merger despite legal problems," *Fort Worth Star-Telegram,* June 22, 1989, section 1, p. 17.

63. Stratton interview.

64. Gammage, "Boys clubs plan to join hands on path into '90s," *Fort Worth Star-Telegram* clipping, no date, pp. 17, 27, in Clippings Box, HVL Collection, FWPL; also Minutes, FWBC Council, Nov. 14, 1989.

65. Mutual Compromise Settlement and Release Agreement December 3, 1991, No. 348-118749-89, FWBC, Inc., vs. Endowment and Council, p. 6, Lawsuit Box, HVL Collection, FWPL; also "Settlement Agreement," Cause No. 348-118749-89, May 13, 1991, between FWBC, Inc., Endowment, and Council, p. 2.

66. Fort Worth Boys' Council, Inc., *Yearbook,* 1990, in "Yearbooks" Box, HVL Collection, FWPL; also Minutes, FWBC Council, Aug. 29, 1989; also Handwritten Minutes of Fort Worth Youth Council, June 1, 1993.

67. Michael Handy, Attorney, letter to Mr. James B. Barlow, Mediator, June 27, 1989, in Lawsuit Box, HVL Collection, FWPL.

68. Gilder, King, and Gregor interviews.

69. Minutes, FWBC Endowment Fund, Inc., Sept. 23, 1992.

CHAPTER 12

1. "Work Copy" of Taped Interview, May 21, 1986, p. 6, at Annual Meeting, BCA, Inc., cut to ten minutes in "Historical Notes" Folder in History Box 1, HVL Collection, FWPL.

2. Bill Brittain, Executive Director, letter to HVL, Mar. 1, 1985, in Correspondence Box, HVL Collection, FWPL.

3. Charlie Ingram, Division Manager, United Way of Metropolitan Tarrant County, letter to HVL, Nov. 17, 1980, in Correspondence Box, HVL Collection, FWPL.

4. Gregor, Kerr and Fogle interviews.

5. Minutes, FWBC Endowment Fund, Inc., Sept. 16, 1981, and notes written later in margin. Actually, the lot on which the building stood is being leased from the Boys' and Girls' Club of Greater Fort Worth, Inc., so the donation must have gone through. Elmer Grammer, lessee, interview by author, Aug. 17, 1998.

6. Bill Burklow, letter to HVL, Aug. 10, 1984, Correspondence Box, HVL Collection, FWPL.

7. Larry Nelson, Vice President Investments, Prudential-Bache Securities, letter to HVL, Feb. 5, 1985, Correspondence Box, HVL Collection, FWPL.

8. George Smith, "Neighbors: Hazel Leigh," Clipping Box, 1940–1969. The clipping's text comments that the Boys' Club "started 50 years ago today," which would make its date February 1, 1985.

9. Invitation to FWBC Council 50th Anniversary Luncheon in Photo Box 3, HVL Collection, FWPL; also "Proclamation," signed by Mayor Bob Bolen, Mar. 26, 1985, proclaiming March 27 as "Fort Worth Boys' Club Council and Founder Mrs. Hazel Vaughn Leigh Day." in Clippings Box, HVL Collection, FWPL; and Bill Burklow, letter to Mrs. Leigh, Mar. 28, 1985, in Correspondence Box 2, HVL Collection, FWPL.

10. Handwritten Fort Worth Boys' Club Council reply to United Way staff comments, in BCA Box, HVL Collection, FWPL.

11. Hazel Vaughn Leigh to FWBC Board of Directors and Trey Shannon, President, no date, in Correspondence Box, HVL Collection, FWPL; also Ronald E. Gilley, President, FWBC, Inc., to HVL, Aug. 1, 1985, in Correspondence Box, Ibid.

12. "3 Initiated Into 50-Year Club At Annual Magnolia Luncheon," *Fort Worth News-Tribune,* June 14, 1985, p. 2B.

13. "Work Copy" of Taped Interview, May 21, 1986, at Annual Meeting, cut to ten minutes, comments, back of p. 6, in HVL handwriting, in "Historical Notes" Folder in History Box 1, HVL Collection, FWPL. She wrote the same thing on another copy, back of p. 7.

14. Samuel Hudson, "Thank-yous are given to generous," *Fort Worth Star-Telegram,* Nov. 11, 1987, section 4, p. 5.

15. HVL, letter to Mrs. Bianca Pastore, Aug. 31, 1988, in Correspondence Box, HVL Collection, FWPL; also Snyder interview.

16. Cordova interview.

17. Bill Hinckley, letter to HVL, May 29, 1989, Correspondence Box 2, HVL Collection, FWPL.

18. Geren, Jr., interview.

19. Cordova interview.

20. *Profiles: The Journal of The Association of Boys' and Girls' Club Professionals* (summer 1990).

21. Joe Cordova, letter to HVL, Feb. 23, 1993, in Correspondence Box, HVL Collection, FWPL.

22. Cordova interview. United Way once was ninety-eight percent, but in the 1990s the rest of the funding came from state and federal grants,

foundation giving, corporate giving, annual fund raisers and an annual campaign. They hosted an annual auction and a Cinco de Mayo Dance for which tickets were sold.

23. Gregor and Hawkins interviews.

24. Smith and Hawkins interviews.

25. Gregor interview.

26. Carter interview.

27. HVL, letter to Fran Chiles, no date, Correspondence Box, HVL Collection, FWPL. Mrs. Chiles spoke to the ladies October 30, 1985, so the letter to thank her followed that date.

28. Robert W. Decker, chairman, Community Foundation of Metropolitan Tarrant County, letter to Hazel Leigh, Aug. 29, 1990, in Correspondence Box 2, HVL Collection, FWPL.

29. *Fort Worth Social Directory 1991-1993,* p. 94.

30. Snyder interview; Sylvester interview, Dec. 1, 1997; and Drummond interview.

31. *Yearbook,* Fort Worth Boys' Council, Inc., 1991, p. 4, Yearbooks Box, HVL Collection, FWPL; Special Warrant Deed, 299.01/6, June 14, 1991, Deeds and Leases Box, HVL Collection, FWPL; and Mutual Compromise Settlement and Release Agreement, May 1991 (Cause No. 348-118749-89) in Hazel Vaughn Leigh Box, HVL Collection, FWPL.

32. Geren, Jr., interview.

33. Wheeler interview.

34. Imogene Pardue, telephone interview by author, Sept. 22, 1997; also Geren, Jr., Smith, and Snyder interviews.

35. Snyder interview.

36. Irma Perez, Chair Recognition Event, Fort Worth Commission on the Status of Women, letter to Hazel Vaughn Leigh, Feb. 12, 1992, Correspondence Box, HVL Collection, FWPL; also Anjetta McQueen, "Granger tops the list of honorees," *Fort Worth Star-Telegram,* Mar. 20, 1992, section A, p. 23. Hazel had signed an agreement on November 1, 1991, to donate her papers to the Fort Worth Public Library, but she would release them gradually over the next four years. Ken Hopkins, telephone interview by author, May 12, 1998.

37. Grammer interview; "Above the Crowd," *Fort Worth Star-Telegram,* Feb. 16, 1992, section D, p. 2.

38. Geren, Jr., interview.

39. Carole A. Chambers, Individual Financial Consultants, Beverly Hills, California, letter to HVL, Feb. 19, 1993, BCA Box, HVL Collection, FWPL; also Joe Cordova, letter to HVL, Feb. 23, 1993, in Correspondence Box, HVL Collection, FWPL.

40. Geren, Jr., interview; Handwritten Application Nomination Form for Fort Worth Historic Preservation Awards Committee, 1993, Hazel Vaughn Leigh Box, HVL Collection, FWPL. Unfortunately, when Hazel died, her furniture and household goods were sold at an estate sale. The old pistol, butter dish, and other items her grandparents and great-grandparents had owned were sold because the bank trust officer managing the sale did not know their history.

41. Geren, Jr., Wheeler, and Snyder interviews; Juanita Vaughn Garrison, interview by author, Fort Worth, Sept. 30, 1998. Juanita's father and Hazel were first cousins.

42. Hopkins interview; Sue McCafferty, President, North Fort Worth Historical Society, letter to HVL, Apr. 6, 1993, in Correspondence Box 2, HVL Collection, FWPL. Hazel saved the invitation.

43. Amy Keen, "Historical society honors North side figures," *Fort Worth Star-Telegram,* Apr. 30, 1993, section A, p. 26.

44. Geren, Jr., Snyder, and Cordova interviews; and Hazel Vaughn Leigh, letter to Fort Worth Boys' Club Endowment Fund Board, Inc., Sept. 1, 1993, copy in possession of author, received from Preston Geren, Jr. The Panther Boys' Club had a couple of endowments named after the people who gave them (Rady and Ballard), which together are worth over $1.5 million.

45. Hazel mentioned an intention to write a book on a handwritten Application Nomination Form for Fort Worth Historic Preservation Awards Committee in 1993, Hazel Vaughn Leigh Box, HVL Collection, FWPL; Nurses Log, June 6 and 22, and Aug. 7, 1994, Nurses Log, Apr. 8, 1995; in possession of author.

46. Geren, Jr., and Wheeler interviews; and Obituary, Marsha Z. Ammons, "Hazel Vaughn Leigh, 97, helped delinquent youths," *Fort Worth Star-Telegram,* Apr. 29, 1995, Vertical File, FWPL.

47. King interview.

48. Christopher Evans, "Personalities For the Boys," *Fort Worth Star-Telegram,* May 31, 1992, section E, p. 5. Also Hazel Vaughn Leigh Estate, Case Number 95-1150-2, Tarrant County Court House p.3

49. Hazel Vaughn Leigh Estate; Geren, Jr., interview.

EPILOGUE

1. Mrs. Morris is the aunt of the author. In August 1999, she was ninety-two years old.

2. Jane Addams, *Twenty Years at Hull-House, with Autobiographical Notes,* pp. 66, 93, 104; also Allen F. Davis and Mary Lynn McCree, *Eighty Years at Hull-House,* p. 6, 143, 145, 213–14; also Brous interview.

3. Fulton Oursler and Will Oursler, *Father Flanagan of Boys Town,* pp. 3, 148, 162, and opposite p. 273.

4. Schmidt, *Fort Worth and Tarrant County,* p. 43.

5. Sarsgard interview.

6. Marti, Roberts, and King interviews.

7. Stratton interview.

8. Caufield interview.

BIBLIOGRAPHY

PRIMARY SOURCES

MANUSCRIPTS AND COLLECTIONS

Fort Worth Public Library. Federal Writer's Project, 70 Vols.: *Research Data, Fort Worth and Tarrant County, Texas.*
Fort Worth Public Library. Hazel Vaughn Leigh Collection.
Fort Worth Public Library. Martha Justice Ball Collection.
Fort Worth Public Library. Mary Daggett Lake Collection.
St. Andrews Episcopal Church. Fort Worth. *Records.* Hazel Vaughn Leigh Confirmation.
University of Texas at Arlington Special Collections. *Fort Worth Star-Telegram* Collection, "Fort Worth Boys' Club," "Hazel Vaughn Leigh," "Panther Boys' Club."

GOVERNMENT DOCUMENTS AND PUBLICATIONS

Azle, Texas. *Minutes of Board of Trustees,* Azle Independent School District. Regular Board Meeting, August 15, 1995.
Bartlesville, Oklahoma. *City Directory,* 1923.
Fort Worth, Texas. *City Directory,* 1926-1945 (1944 missing).
San Francisco, California. *City Directory,* 1925.
State of Texas. Certificate of Death. Hazel Vaughn Leigh.
Tarrant County Court House. Grover C. Leigh Estate.
Tarrant County Court House. Hazel Vaughn Leigh Estate.

CORRESPONDENCE

Gonzales, Alberto R., Secretary of State, to author, October 12, 1998.
Inman, Kimberly, Bartlesville Public Library, to author, August 16, 1997.
Kingman, Joyce Chambers, to author, September 24, 1997.
Landazuri, Roberto, Librarian, San Francisco History Center, to author, February 4, 1998.
Nurses' Notes, Hazel Vaughn Leigh Care, May 29, 1994, through April 13, 1995.

INTERVIEWS

Baldwin, Kay Fortson. Fort Worth. November 25, 1997.
Ball, Graham. Wichita Falls. September 30, 1997.

Bell, Carman. Hot Springs Village, Arkansas. September 30, 1998.

Brous, Michie. Fort Worth. November 19, 1997.

Burklow, Bill. Houston. August 17, 1998.

Carpenter, Tim. Azle, Texas. August, 7, 1997.

Carter, Buddy. Fort Worth. October 9, 1997.

Caufield, Jim. Atlanta, Georgia. August 17, 1998.

Chambers, Mrs. Charles Robert. Fort Worth. September 30, 1998.

Clark, D. C. Fort Worth. May 20, 1998.

Cordova, Joe. Fort Worth. September 29, 1997.

Derrett, Delbert. Hurst, Texas. September 5, 1997.

Derrick, Fay Dell. San Angelo. August 13, 1997.

Drummond, Kris. Fort Worth, November 12, 1997.

Duncan, Betty. Duncanville, Texas. August 2, 1997.

Dunn, Henson. Azle, Texas. August 7, 1997.

Fogle, Beverly. Fort Worth. July 27, 1998.

Forte, Santo. Azle, Texas. July 31, 1997.

Garrison, Juanita Vaughn. Fort Worth. September 30, 1998.

Geren, Preston, Jr. Fort Worth. October 21, 1997.

Gibson, Wanda. Fort Worth. August 4, 1998.

Gilder, Muriel. Fort Worth. December 12, 1997.

Gilley, Ron. Fort Worth. September 25, 1998.

Goodger, Miller. Fort Worth. September 25, 1997.

Grammer, Elmer. Fort Worth. August 17, 1998.

Graves, Gene. Fort Worth. September 24, 1998.

Graves, Nita. Fort Worth. September 28, 1998.

Gregor, Nelda. Fort Worth. December 9, 1997.

Haas, Ken. Azle, Texas. August 15, 1997.

Hawkins, Gloria Davis. Fort Worth. April 24 and August 20, 1998.

Hopkins, Ken. Fort Worth. May 12, 1998.

Jenkins, Nancy Duncan. El Paso. August 2, 1997, and February 21, 1998.

Johnson, Paul. Fort Worth. December 4, 1997.

Jones, Martha. Boyd. August 27, 1998.

Kerr, Ruby. El Paso. February 23, 1998.

King, Virginia. Fort Worth. February 20, 1998.

Kingston, Joyce. Austin. September 22, 1997.

Koeppe, Paul. Fort Worth. September 24, 1997.

Lawrence, Edward M. Fort Worth. February 15, 1999.

Leigh, Hazel Vaughn. Oral Histories of Fort Worth, Inc., Sponsored by Junior League, Interview by Joanne Pettit. July 22, 1977.

Machos, Bob. River Oaks, Texas. September 15, 1997.

Makarwich, C. C. "Corky." River Oaks. Texas. September 11, 1997.

Marti, Michelle. Cleburne. September 20, 1997.

Martinez, Mary Anna. Fort Worth. October 1, 1998.

McCafferty, Sue. Fort Worth. May 12, 1998.

McClellan, Ray. Azle, Texas. August 15, 1997.

Neal, Orville, Fort Worth. February 19 and September 21, 1998.

Olien, Diana. Odessa, Texas. April 2, 1998.

O'Neill, Walter. Fort Worth. September 30, 1998.

Pardue, Imogene. Fort Worth. September 22, 1997.

Petruccelli, Ann. Fort Worth. July 28, 1998.

Powell, Mary Mann. Gardendale, Texas. August 15, 1997.

Pressley, Julian "Snooky." Odessa. July 17, 1997.

Ramos, Sergio. Fort Worth. August 25, 1998.

Roberts, Lesbia. Fort Worth. September 16 and Oct. 24, 1997

Sarsgard, William. Fort Worth. July 29, 1998.

Shannon, J. O. "Trey" III. Fort Worth. September 17, 1997.

Sharpe, Aubrey. Tyler. September 22, 1997.

Shinn, Gerald. Azle, Texas. July 29, 1997.

Smith, Mary. Fort Worth. October 3, 1997.

Snyder, Eileen. Fort Worth. February 6, 1998.

Stratton, Jim. Scottsdale, Arizona. July 27, 1998.

Sylvester, Mona. Fort Worth. December 1, 1997, and January. 26, 1998.

Trammell, Audrey, Azle, Texas. September 6, 1997.

Westfall, Marla. Fort Worth. September 8, 1997.

Wheeler, Barbara. Fort Worth. October 6, 1997.

Wilson, Judy. Fort Worth. October 27, 1997, May 13 and July 27, 1998.

Wilson, Raymond "Tuffy." Arlington. September 21, 1998.

NEWSPAPERS AND PERIODICALS

The Azle News

Fort Worth News-Tribune

Fort Worth Press

Fort Worth Star-Telegram

North Fort Worth News

SECONDARY SOURCES

BOOKS

Addams, Jane. *Twenty Years at Hull-House, with Autobiographical Notes.* New York: The Macmillan Company, 1910.

Allen, Frederick Lewis. *Only Yesterday: An Informal History of the 1920s.* New York: Harper & Row, Publishers, 1931; reprint 1959, 1964.

Andrist, Ralph K. ed. *The American Heritage History of the 20s & 30s.* New York: American Heritage Publishing Co., Inc., 1970.

Annual. Central High School. Fort Worth, 1914.

Atkinson, R. K. *The Boys' Club.* New York: Association Press, 1939.

Beane, Wilhemina. *Texas Thirties.* San Antonio: The Naylor Company, 1963.

Carter, Paul. *The Twenties in America.* New York: Thomas Y. Crowell Company, 1968.

Davis, Allen F. and Mary Lynn McCree. *Eighty Years at Hull-House.* Chicago: Quadrangle Books, 1969.

Durant, John and Alice. *Pictoral History of American Presidents.* New York: A. S. Barnes and Company, 1955.

Falls, Roy E. *A Fascinating Biography of J. Frank Norris.* Euless, Texas: Roy Emerson Falls, 1975.

Farman, Irvin. *Tandy's Money Machine.* Chicago: Mobrium Press, 1992.

Flamm, Jerry. *Good Life in Hard Times.* San Francisco: Chronicle Books, 1977.

_____. *Hometown San Francisco Sunny Jim, Phat Willie, and Dave.* San Francisco: Scottwall Associates, 1994.

Flemmons, Jerry. *Amon: the Life of Amon Carter, Sr., of Texas.* Austin: Jenkins Publishing Company, 1978.

Fort Worth Social Directory 1991–1993. Fort Worth: Kay Fortson Baldwin, Ben Fortson, III, Publishers, 1991.

Gould, Lewis L., ed. *The Progressive Era.* Syracuse, New York: Syracuse University Press, 1974.

Hall, William Edwin. *100 Years and Millions of Boys: The Dynamic Story of the Boys' Clubs of America.* New York: Farrar, Straus and Cudahy, 1961.

Hamill, James M. *The Major and His Boys: The Story of Major Sidney Peixotto and the Columbia Park Boys' Club.* Los Angeles: Anderson, Ritchie and Simon, 1972.

The Horned Frog, Texas Christian University Annual, 1915, 1916, 1918.

Issel, William and Robert W. Cherney. *San Francisco 1865–1932: Politics, Power, and Urban Development.* Berkeley: University of California Press, 1986.

Jary, William E., Jr. *Camp Bowie, Fort Worth: 1917–18.* Fort Worth: B. B. Maxfield Foundation, 1975.

Knight, Oliver. *Fort Worth: Outpost on the Trinity, with an Essay on the Twentieth Century by Cissy Stewart Lale.* Norman: University of Oklahoma Press, 1953; reprint, Fort Worth: Texas Christian University Press, 1990.

Leuchtenburg, William E. *The Perils of Prosperity: 1914–32.* Chicago: The University of Chicago Press, 1958; reprint, 1973.

Magnus, Werner. *Who Was Hulen?* Fort Worth: Bill Hanson Printing, Inc., 1990.

Mowry, George E., ed. *The Twenties: Fords, Flappers and Fanatics.* Englewood Cliffs, New Jersey: Prentice-Hall, Inc., 1963.

Myres, Sandra L., ed. *Force Without Fanfare: The Autobiography of K. M. Van Zandt.* Fort Worth: Texas Christian University Press, 1968, second printing, 1995.

1934 Year Book of the Boys Clubs of America, Inc. New York: BCA, Inc., 1934.

Oil Legends of Fort Worth. The Historical Committee of The Fort Worth Petroleum Club. Fort Worth: Taylor Publishing Company, 1993.

Oursler, Fulton and Will. *Father Flanagan Of Boys Town.* Garden City, New York: Doubleday & Company, Inc., 1949.

Page, Thomas. *San Francisco.* San Francisco: Minerva Editions, 1977.

Pate, J'Nell L. *Livestock Legacy: The Fort Worth Stockyards, 1887–1987.* College Station: Texas A&M University Press, 1988.

_____. *North of the River: A Brief History of North Fort Worth.* Fort Worth: Texas Christian University Press, 1994.

Pirtle, Caleb III. *Fort Worth: The Civilized West.* Tulsa, Oklahoma: Continental Heritage Press, Inc., 1980.

Porter, Roze McCoy. *Thistle Hill: The Cattle Baron's Legacy.* Fort Worth: Branch-Smith, Inc., 1980.

Race, Lila Bunch. *Pioneer Fort Worth, Texas: Life, Times and Families of South Tarrant County.* Fort Worth: Taylor Publishing Co., 1976.

Reynolds, Clay. *A Hundred Years of Heroes. A History of the Southwestern Exposition and Livestock Show.* Fort Worth: Texas Chrstian University Press, 1995.

Roark, Carol. *Fort Worth's Legendary Landmarks.* Fort Worth: Texas Christian University Press, 1995.

Sanders, Leonard and Ronnie C. Tyler. *How Fort Worth Became the Texasmost City.* Fort Worth: Amon Carter Museum of Western Art, 1973.

Schmelzer, Janet. *Where the West Begins: Fort Worth and Tarrant County.* North Ridge, California: Windsor Publications, 1985.

Schmidt, Ruby. *Fort Worth and Tarrant County: A Historical Guide.* Fort Worth: Texas Christian University Press, 1984.

Selcer, Richard F. *The Fort That Became A City: An Illustrated Reconstruction of Fort Worth, Texas, 1849-1853.* Fort Worth: Texas Christian University Press, 1995.

Shannon, David A. *Between the Wars: America, 1919-1941.* Boston: Houghton Mifflin Company, 1965.

_____. *The Great Depression.* Englewood Cliffs, New Jersey: Prentice-Hall, 1960.

Talbert, Robert H. *Cowtown Metropolis: Case Study of a City's Growth and Structure.* Fort Worth: Leo Potishman Foundation, Texas Christian University, 1956.

Teague, Margaret Withers. *History of Washington County and Surrounding Areas.* Bartlesville, Oklahoma: Bartlesville Historical Commission, 1967.

Wecter, Dixon. *The Age of the Great Depression, 1929–1941.* Lexington, Mass.: The Macmillan Company, 1948.

Williamson, Harold F., Ralph L. Andreano, Arnold R. Daum, and Gilbert C. Klose. *The American Petroleum Industry: The Age of Energy, 1899–1959.* Evanston: Northwestern University Press, 1963.

ARTICLES

"George Bush: The American Spirit of Voluntarism Alive and Well in Boys' Clubs." *Connections: The Quarterly Magazine of Boys' Clubs of America* (summer 1982): 3–5.

Hughes, Mrs. Edwin H., "The Women's Auxiliary and Communications," *The Journal: Boys' Clubs of America* 3:4 (fall 1968): 39–41.

"To Have And To Hold: Managing Club Endowments." *Connections: The Quarterly Magazine of Boys' Clubs of America* (spring 1987): 9–11.

PAMPHLETS

Boys and Girls Clubs of America. Packet of Pamphlets and Brochures: "The Positive Place for Kids: Investing in America's Future," "The Carnegie Report," "Youth Development: The Foundation For the Future," "Safe Havens to learn . . . to grow . . . to be."

"Boys and Girls Clubs of Greater Dallas: A History of Service." one page sheet.

Boys and Girls Clubs of Greater Fort Worth. Packet of Pamphlets and Brochures: "Join the Club!" "Educational Talent Search," "Smart Moves," "Teen Drama," "Comin' Up: A Youth Gang Intervention Program," "Want to Do Something about the Problems in Our Community? Join the Club!"

THESES

Eastin, Gregory Mark. "Social Agency Transportation Services for the Disadvantaged: A Case Study of Fort Worth, Texas." Master's Thesis, University of Texas at Arlington, 1976.

Flemmons, Jerry. "Amon: The Man Who Invented the Cowboy," Unpublished manuscript, revision of earlier book.

Henderson, Donald Alvin. "Fort Worth and the Depression 1929–1933." Master's Thesis, Texas Christian University, 1964.

Keaveney, Sister Mary Ailbe. "The Depression Era in Fort Worth, Texas 1929–1934." Master's Thesis, University of Texas at Austin, 1974.

Porter, Fred Baker. "Indices of Social Organization and Disorganization in Fort Worth by Areas As Related To The Problems of Youth." Master's Thesis, Texas Christian University, 1946.

INDEX

References to individuals or events in photographs are indicated by italics.

Meacham, Mrs. H.C., 53

meat-packing. *See* Armour and Co. *or* Swift and Co.

medical aid (FWBC). *See* Greines, Dr. Abe *or* Calkins, Dr. Russell, Jr.

Mexicans, 42, 78, 98–99. See also racial tensions

Michie, Mrs., 99

military, Camp Bowie, 12; Leigh, Grover 16–17; Machos, Bob 70; Snow, Otis 72, 75; Vaughn, Howard 12, *13*. See also World War II

Mills, Mr. J.E., 47, 56

Mineral Wells (Texas), 22–23

Minor, C.S., *39*

minority membership (FWBC), 101, 109. See also specific entries: African Americans, Hispanics, Mexicans; racial tensions

model airplane contest, 67; *68*

Moncrief, W.A. ("Monty"), 21

Monnig, William N., Sr., 53

Monnig's Department Store, 47

Moore, M.H., 28

Morris, Judge Walter, 61

Morris, Marjorie, 135

Municipal Airport (Meacham Field), 67

national boys' club movement. *See* boys' club

National Boys' Club. *See* Boys' Club of America *or* Campbell, Alexander

National Boys' Club Federation, 26, 33

National Boys' Club Week (March), 78, 84

National Supply Company, 15, 79

National Womens' Committee on the Mobilization for Human Needs, 31

National Youth Administration, 50, 63; withdrawal of aid to FWBC, 71

National Youth Week (April), 47

NBCF. *See* National Boys' Club Federation

Negroes. *See* African Americans

Nelson, Larry Wayne (former FWBC member), 124

News Boys' Club. *See* Panther Boys' Club

New Isis Theatre, 45, 58. See also Tidball, Louis

'93 Club, 96, 130

Nolan, Miss, 72

Northern Traction Company, 27

Norris, Reverend J. Frank, 12, 14, 31

NYA. *See* National Youth Administration

Odessa (Texas), Boys' Club, 135

oil boom cities, 15

oil equipment. *See* National Supply Company or Empire Oil

Owens, B.W. Lumber Company, 61

Owens, Margaret, 95

Panther Boys' Club, 25, 26, 27, 28–29; benefactors, 81; camp, 103; directors, 33, 75, 91, 115; discipline problems, 51; expansion, 106; Ladies' Auxiliary of, 25, 27, 29, 57; membership, 57; merger with FWBC, 119–121, 126–127; review show, 28; support from Rotary Club, 77, 79; thefts from, 32–34. See also Boys' and Girls' Club of Greater Fort Worth

Papineau, Genevieve, 22

Patterson, C.C., 48

Peden, Les, 105

Peixotto, Major Sidney, 20

population: Fort Worth, 15, 31, 38; Texas counties, 32

Pressley, Julian ("Snooky"), *39*, 60, 75, 137; correspondence with Hazel, 65, 75

Price Boys' Club. *See* Panther Boys' Club

About the Author

✤✤✤✤✤✤✤✤✤✤✤✤✤✤✤✤✤✤✤✤✤✤✤✤✤✤✤✤✤✤✤

J'Nell Pate, a long-time resident of the Fort Worth area, is professor of history at Tarrant County College. Mrs. Pate has published extensively, including a regular column "Pages from Western History" for the *Azle News,* as well as scholarly articles and book reviews. She is the author of *Livestock Legacy* (Texas A&M University Press) and *North of the River: A Brief History of North Fort Worth* (TCU Press). Pate is a fellow of the Texas State Historical Association.